# NIC

# LO
# MUSEUMS
*&*
# GALLERIES
# GUIDE

**Andrew Duncan**

Nicholson

*An Imprint of Bartholomew*
*A Division of* HarperCollins*Publishers*

A Nicholson Guide

First published 1992
Copyright © Nicholson 1992

Photographs by Oliver Hewitt on pages 59, 95, 106, 119, 120, 137, 160
Photographs by Nick Daly on pages 15, 63, 92, 122, 145, 167

All photographs © Nicholson except the following, which are reproduced
by kind permission of the copyright holders:
p9 Bank of England Museum courtesy of the Governor and the Company
of the Bank of England; p11 Banqueting House Crown copyright (PSA
Photographic Services); p20 Cabinet War Rooms; p29 Geffrye Museum
© Geffrye Museum Trust; p32 HMS *Belfast* © Imperial War Museum;
p38 Livesey Museum; p44 Madame Tussaud's; p50 Museum of London;
p75 Royal Air Force Museum; p83 Science Museum; p93 Tower Bridge
Museum; p99 Victoria & Albert Museum; p110 Church Farm House
Museum © Dept of Libraries and Arts, London Borough of Barnet;
p112 Dickens House; p115 Freud Museum, photographed by Nick
Bagguley; p148 National Portrait Gallery; p154 Saatchi Collection,
photograph by courtesy of Anthony Oliver; p165 Kew Gardens Gallery,
© A. McRobb, Royal Botanic Gardens; p169 Small Mansion Art Gallery,
photographed by Michael Harris; p174 Hampstead Museum; p178 Vestry
House Museum, London Borough of Waltham Forest.

Floor plans © Nicholson
by Rodney Paull

Maps © Nicholson, generated from the Bartholomew London Digital
Database

London Underground Map reproduced by permission of London Regional
Transport. LRT Registered User No. 92/1496

Nicholson
HarperCollins*Publishers*
77-85 Fulham Palace Road
Hammersmith
London W6 8JB

Great care has been taken throughout this book to be accurate, but the
publishers cannot accept responsibility for any errors which appear, or their
consequences.

Printed in Hong Kong

ISBN 0 7028 1752 X    92/1/110    LNU

# *CONTENTS*

| | |
|---|---|
| **Introduction** | 5 |
| **MUSEUMS** | 7 |
| **HISTORIC HOUSE MUSEUMS** | 107 |
| **ART COLLECTIONS** | 140 |
| **EXHIBITION GALLERIES** | 159 |
| **LOCAL HISTORY MUSEUMS** | 171 |
| **Index of Local History Museums** | 179 |
| **Index of Artists and Craftsmen** | 180 |
| **Index** | 187 |
| **Street Maps** | 193 |
| **Underground Map** | 208 |

## Acknowledgements

Thanks to my good friends Helena Beaufoy, Jeremy Finnis, Wendy Palmer and particularly Anthony Terry for all their help with this book.

This book is dedicated to my parents.

Andrew Duncan 1992

Andrew Duncan is a professional historian and guidebook writer, with a great interest in museums. Brought up in Yorkshire and educated at Oxford University, his academic qualifications include a first class degree in history and a doctorate for research on the 18th century. He has lived in London for several years and spends much of his time exploring its highways and byways, and writing books and articles about its history and numerous attractions.

### How to use this guide

All entries are listed alphabetically within their sections and have a map reference which refers to the colour street maps at the back of the book. At the end of each entry is a box with useful information to help you get the most out of your visit. This includes opening times; whether or not there is an admission charge; availability of guided tours (for which you often need to book in advance), guidebooks and films; shops; education programmes; refreshment facilities*; disabled/wheelchair access (partial access usually means there will be steps to be negotiated); and the nearest Underground/British Rail station or bus route.

*The following symbols and abbreviations are used in the guide*:

$\ominus$ = Underground station

$\rightleftarrows$ = British Rail station

$\boxed{\&}$ = disabled/wheelchair access

* opening times for refreshment facilities are only given when they vary significantly from those of the museum or gallery; otherwise assume restaurants/cafés will be open similar hours but usually starting $^{1}/_{h}$-hour after doors open and ending $^{1}/_{h}$-hour before closing.

# *INTRODUCTION*

Among London's many attractions, the museums and galleries really stand out. It has more of them than any other city in the world, and the biggest and best of them are in a class of their own.

Why is London so blessed in this respect? Perhaps it's something to do with the fact that the largest and richest of all – the British Museum – is also the oldest, founded in 1753 when there was hardly another museum in the whole country, let alone London. The BM set a precedent for museum-founding which governments, private collectors and all manner of organisations from companies to sports stadiums have followed over the years. Even in these days of reductions in public expenditure, new museums are still opening all the time – a great tribute to the boundless enthusiasm and energy of the people concerned in getting new projects off the ground.

Today the number of London's museums and galleries tops 200. In this new Nicholson guide we describe everything from the great national collections like the Victoria & Albert and Science museums, with their miles of galleries, right down to the very smallest private museums, consisting perhaps of just a handful of display cases. Among the art collections we include nearly 40 exhibition galleries (those which do not have their own permanent collections) where you can see the very best in contemporary (and sometimes historical) art in all media.

Many of these galleries and museums are in proper museum buildings or in the kinds of historic buildings you would expect: country houses, royal palaces, great churches and cathedrals. But many more are in totally unexpected places such as hospitals, schools, universities, trade unions, learned societies, banks, ships, shops, bridges, railway stations, army barracks, windmills and private homes. There's even one in a pub! These immensely varied locations add enormously to the pleasure of visiting museums in London.

Whichever attractions you choose to visit, and the choice is vast, you will see great paintings and works of art, fascinating historical relics, pioneering inventions, the wonders of nature, shrines to famous people, gems of architecture and interior design, and fine examples of crafts and cultures of people from all parts of the world and throughout human history. One of the great marvels of London's museums is how much they can teach us, not only about London and Britain, but about the rest of the world as well.

The primary purpose of museums is, of course, to educate. Each one you go to will tell you something you did not know before. But museums should also entertain – indeed they must if they are to attract the numbers of people they need in order to survive. More and more museums are coming to accept this – even the old-fashioned, traditionally rather fusty ones. With their interactive exhibits, unusual shops and high-quality restaurants, many London museums, particularly the bigger ones and those unburdened by serious academic pretensions, now compete on equal, if not better, terms with more obvious entertainment attractions and provide really enthralling days out for people of all ages and interests.

Going to a museum sounds like a pretty straightforward process, but there are potential pitfalls. Here are some tips on how to avoid disappointment and make your visit more enjoyable:

1. For all sorts of reasons, museums can be forced to close at unadvertised times, sometimes for long periods. *Always phone before your visit to be on the safe side.*

2. Many museums either shut their doors or pull the plug on working exhibits before the advertised closing times. *Make sure you arrive early.*

3. Few museums and galleries are entirely static. Most are continually acquiring new things or improving on the way they show their collections. Some will also rotate the exhibits because of lack of space. *If there is something you particularly want to see, phone first to make sure it is on view.*

4. In addition, several museums now operate 'Friends' schemes offering their members free admission, special events, private views, club rooms and other privileges. If you have a favourite museum or gallery, this is an ideal way of supporting it.

# *MUSEUMS*

### Alfred Dunhill Collection

30 Duke Street SW1. 071-499 9566 x 2033.    4 D4

Alfred Dunhill founded the famous tobacco and gentlemen's accessories firm in 1907. As a sideline he collected pipes both antique and curious from all over the world. The 240-piece collection is now displayed in a room above his original shop in Duke Street, St James's. Spanning three centuries, it includes everything from Indian peace pipes and opium pipes, to pipes with interesting historical associations, such as those belonging to the Duke of Windsor. Two highlights are the huge commemorative Meerschaum made to celebrate the marriage of one of Queen Victoria's daughters to the Marquis of Lorne in 1871, and a rare carved slate pipe, with a bear holding the bowl, from Queen Charlotte Island in British Columbia.

Dunhill's have a second collection in a room above their other central London shop at 60-61 Burlington Arcade, Piccadilly W1 (4 D3). 071-499 9566 x 2033. *Open by appointment only 09.30-16.00 Mon-Fri.* Admission free. This shows some of the ingenious lighters, elegant watches, gold pens, jewel-encrusted cigarette cases and other personal luxury goods which have made the name of Dunhill synonymous with style and quality over the past 80 years. Interestingly the collection also contains some of the motoring accessories such as leather coats, dust coats and motoring trunks which Alfred Dunhill sold before making his name as a purveyor of personally-blended tobaccos.

---

**Alfred Dunhill Collection**
*Open 09.30-17.30 Mon-Fri, 09.30-16.00 Sat.* Admission free.
&#9855; Full access. Toilet.
&#9903; Piccadilly Circus

---

### All-Hallows-by-the-Tower Undercroft Museum

Byward Street EC3. 071-481 2928.    5 F3

This historic church near the Tower of London was built in Saxon times over Roman foundations. The small museum in the undercroft contains a section of Roman pavement and some excavated Roman artefacts, a model of Roman London, and some Saxon carvings. In the small chapel at the end of the museum there is a medieval crusaders' altar brought back from Jerusalem. Also on show are several pieces of the church's plate, and two of its parish registers: one is open at the baptism of William Penn, founder of Pennsylvania; the other at the marriage of John Quincy Adams, sixth president of the United States.

---

**All-Hallows-by-the-Tower Undercroft Museum**
*Open by appointment only 10.00-17.30 Mon-Fri, to 16.30 Sat & Sun.*
Admission charge.
Guided tours, guidebook.
*Educational facilities*: Tours for schools, children's guidebook.
&#x267f; No access
&#x2296; Tower Hill

---

## Amalgamated Engineering Union Collection

110 Peckham Road, Peckham SE15. 071-703 4231.
Opened in 1984 by the leader of the Labour Party, Neil Kinnock, this one-room museum in the Union's headquarters covers the history of the Union back to its origins in the 1820s. In the display cases are many examples of the kinds of things members of the Union have made over the past century or so. They range from an old 'boneshaker' bicycle, with wooden wheels, to the Rolls Royce Merlin engine that powered the Spitfire and other famous aircraft of World War II.

---

**Amalgamated Engineering Union Collection**
*Open by appointment only 09.30-17.00 Mon-Fri.* Admission free.
&#x267f; Partial access
&#x2296; Oval (then bus 36)

---

## Baden-Powell House

65-67 Queen's Gate SW7. 071-584 7031.                    3 D6
At this international hostel for scouts and guides on the corner of Queen's Gate and Cromwell Road, there is a small exhibition on the ground floor of the foyer called the B-P Story. As its name suggests, it is about the life and times of Robert Baden-Powell (1857-1941), the founder of the boy scout and girl guide movements. The story is told mainly through words and pictures, but there are a few scouting, guiding and Baden-Powell exhibits (such as his dress uniform and medals) and also some interesting relics of the siege of Mafeking, one of the most famous actions of the Boer War. B-P's heroic defence of the town, during which boys were used as

messengers and in other important roles, made him a national hero and sowed in his mind the first seeds of the scouting movement.

> **Baden-Powell House**
> *Open 07.00-20.30 Mon-Sun.* Admission free.
> Guided tours.
> *Educational facilities*: Tours for schools, worksheets.
> &#9855; Full access
> &#1086; Gloucester Road, South Kensington

### Bank of England Museum
Threadneedle Street EC2. 071-601 5545.   5 E2
Built as the Bank Stock Office by Sir John Soane (architect to the Bank 1788-1833) in the late 18thC, the original museum stood exactly on this spot until a comprehensive rebuilding masterminded by Sir Herbert Baker between the wars. It came to its site here in Threadneedle Street in 1734 and was nicknamed 'The Old Lady of Threadneedle Street' after an MP referred to it as 'an elderly lady of great credit and long standing'.

Although the City has been very much in the public eye

*Bank of England*

since Big Bang and the great privatisation share issues of the 1980s, few people outside know what really goes on there. You can find out about the banking part by visiting the Bank of England's excellent and lavishly-presented museum, opened in 1988. It includes an interactive video system showing how the Bank and the modern banking system works, and a dealing desk similar to the ones used by the Bank's real dealers. A commentary on the telephone explains what the screens show and how the Gilts and other markets work.

Before you reach the dealing desk, numbered displays focus on important events in the Bank's long history and show how it has evolved from a private bank, established in 1694, into a nationalised central bank at the heart of one of the world's great financial centres. The Bank's own history is cleverly tied in to the wider history of banking and there are displays on general themes such as the history of the gold standard, established in 1816. Gold bullion bars, bank notes, forgeries, early note-printing machinery, paintings and prints are exhibited, together with historic documents which include the original proposal for the bank by Scottish merchant William Paterson, and the book recording the names of those who subscribed to the Bank's original £1.2m loan capital.

The museum has gone to great lengths to create spaces for its displays which resemble original rooms in the Bank. The most impressive is the first: a large stone-floored hall with counters all the way round, a glowing fire, and figures dressed in period costume.

---

**Bank of England Museum**

*Open Easter-Sep 10.00-17.00 Mon-Fri, 11.00-17.00 Sat, Sun & Bank Hols: Oct-Easter 10.00-17.00 Mon-Fri only.* Admission free. Shop. Guided tours. Sound guide. Guidebook. Films. Research facilities.

*Educational facilities*: Tours, worksheets, lectures, workshops.

♿ Partial access. Some difficult steps.

⊖ Bank

---

### Banqueting House

Whitehall SW1. 071-930 4179.                                    4 F4

The only remaining part of Whitehall Palace (which burnt down in 1698), the Banqueting House is a large, sumptuously decorated hall built in the early 17thC by Inigo Jones for royal banquets and court ceremonies. Apart from its size, its main feature is a magnificent ceiling painted in the 1630s by Rubens. On January 30 1649, Charles I was executed outside

*Banqueting House*

the Banqueting House (which is opposite Horse Guards) having stepped through one of its high windows onto the scaffold.

> **Banqueting House**
> *Open 10.00-17.00 Mon-Sat. May close at short notice for Government functions.* Admission charge.
> Sales desk. Sound guide (price included with admission ticket).
> Guidebook.
> *Educational facilities*: Tours for schools.
> 🚫 No access
> ⊖ Charing Cross

### Bethnal Green Museum of Childhood
Cambridge Heath Road, Bethnal Green EC2. 081 980 3204.
The Bethnal Green Museum of Childhood is the children's part of the Victoria and Albert Museum. Being an offshoot of the national museum of art and design, it naturally tends to concentrate on the art, craft and design of things made for children. But this emphasis is changing as the upstairs part of the museum is gradually transformed into a comprehensive display on the social history of childhood, putting into context

the museum's wonderful collection of things adults have made for children over the past 300 years. At the moment the upstairs galleries feature learning toys, wedding dresses and children's clothes dating from the 18thC.

By far the largest part of the museum's collection is on the ground floor. Judging by the number and clamour of children visitors, the most popular things are here too! The dolls come in all shapes, sizes and ages: one or two date from as early as the 17thC, but most are 19thC and 20thC. Arranged more or less chronologically, they form a pretty comprehensive survey of doll production in Europe and North America over the past century and a half. Beyond the main doll displays are ethnic dolls from many countries, toy soldiers in a mock fort, space toys, and fascinating early board games, including, inevitably, some overtly moral Victorian examples.

The main toy collection – the largest in Europe – starts with a section on traditional German toys because it was in Germany that mass-production of toys first started. After that the toys are arranged not in chronological order, but by type, with such categories as automata, optical and soft toys. Also lots of teddy bears and rocking horses, though unfortunately nothing for little hands to play with.

Down the central mall you will find the museum's wonderful group of forty-odd dolls' houses, dating from the 18thC, with some complete down to the last pewter tankard in the kitchen. Then, finally, are the puppets and toy theatres. The puppets are, in fact, among the most interesting things in the whole museum and certainly should not be missed just because they are furthest from the door.

---

**Bethnal Green Museum of Childhood**
*Open 10.00-18.00 Mon-Thur & Sat, 14.30-18.00 Sun. Closed May Day Bank Hol.* Admission free.
Shop. Guidebook. Research facilities.
*Educational facilities:* Tours for schools, worksheets, workshops, room available for eating packed lunches.
♿ Partial. Some difficult steps. Help provided if advance notice given.
⊖ Bethnal Green

---

## Black Cultural Museum

378 Coldharbour Lane, Brixton SW9. 071-738 4591.
The Black Cultural Museum is the first of its kind in Britain. Part of a projected archive, museum and cultural centre, its aim is to throw some long-overdue light on Black history in

Britain and Europe, and on the contribution Black people have made to British society. Opened in October 1990, its collection is still small, but there is an active acquisitions programme so new items are being added all the time. On show are books, prints, maps and other primary sources documenting the Black experience. Special collections include musical scores by Samuel Coleridge-Taylor and a set of Caribbean slave papers.

---

**Black Cultural Museum**
*Open 14.00-16.00 Mon, Wed & Fri*. Admission free.
Bookshop *open 10.00-18.00*. Films. Research facilities.
*Educational facilities*: Tours for schools, worksheets, lectures, workshops.
⟨占⟩ Full access. Toilet.
⊖ Brixton

---

## Boxing Museum

Thomas-à-Becket Public House, 320 Old Kent Road, Bermondsey SE1. 071-703 7334.

The Thomas-à-Becket is a famous south London pub with a gym above in which many of the great modern fighters have trained, including Henry Cooper and Muhammad Ali. The walls of both pub and gym are covered in boxing memorabilia – mainly photographs of boxers and matches, and posters advertising fights. In the gym you can also see plaster casts of the hands of famous boxers, and the odd item of clothing, such as the tartan shorts worn by Ken Buchanan when he won the world lightweight championship in the early 1970s. Downstairs in the pub, panels above the bar display 'did-you-know'-type facts and figures from the boxing world. Did you know, for example, that Muhammad Ali won $69 million in his 21-year career? Or that he is the only fighter in history to have recaptured a world title twice? If not, visit the museum.

---

**Boxing Museum**
Pub section *open 12.00-15.00 Mon-Sun*. Gym section *open by appointment only*. Admission free.
*Refreshments*: Hot & cold bar food available all day in pub.
⟨占⟩ Partial access – pub only.
⊖ Elephant & Castle

---

## British Dental Association Museum

64 Wimpole Street W1. 071-935 0875.                    4 C2

A small dental museum in a split-level room in the BDA's headquarters near Harley Street. In the lower gallery there are two reconstructed surgeries, one dating from 1860 and the other from 1899. The difference between the two is quite striking and shows the great advance made in dental science and technology in the intervening 40 years, during which time the BDA was founded. Also down here are various pieces of anaesthetic and X-ray equipment, and a dozen or so dentists' chairs showing their development from the crude barber-dentist chair of the 16thC.

Upstairs is the main collection of dental instruments and equipment. There are fearsome extraction implements such as elevators and root screws dating from the 17thC, and many examples of dentures and old filling materials. Old prints portray with nerve-tingling realism what a horrible business dentistry was in the days before anaesthetics and properly-qualified practitioners.

---

**British Dental Association Museum**
*Open 09.00-17.00 Mon-Fri.* Admission free.
Lectures.
&#9855; No access
&#9758; Oxford Circus

---

### British Museum
Great Russell Street WC1. 071-636 1555.                 1 G6
When wealthy physician and collector Sir Hans Sloane died in 1753, he left his works of art, antiquities and natural history collections to the nation, provided £20,000 was paid for them. The Government wisely put up the money – less than half what Sloane had expended – and, having added two great libraries, the Harleian and the Cottonian, opened the British Museum in 1759. Since then the museum has grown into the largest and finest of its kind in the world, and has been rebuilt or added to many times to house its ever expanding contents. Its most impressive architectural feature, the massive classical Greek facade, was built to designs by Robert Smirke in the 1840s.

The British Museum is British to the extent that it is owned by Britain and stands on British soil, but in terms of its contents – the works of man from prehistoric times to the present day – it really is a world museum. Here you can see and study artefacts both useful and/or decorative produced by every important culture in the world, or at least originating in every major geographical region of the world. An important point to note at this juncture is that at present the museum's ethnographical collections, covering Africa, Australasia, the

Pacific Islands and the Americas, form a separate museum, the Museum of Mankind in Mayfair. The collections had to be moved in 1970 due to lack of space, but will return to the BM during the 1990s when the British Library moves out to its new premises. Strictly speaking, the British Library is separate from the British Museum, but while it continues to share the same building, it is, for the purposes of visitors, all one and the same (there is a chance to see the famous circular domed reading room where Marx wrote *Das Capital*, *on the hour every hour between 11.00-16.00*).

In the vast BM, where everything – including many of the exhibits – is on a monumental scale, there are nearly 100 galleries. Here you will see a huge variety of objects, including statues, carvings, reliefs, sculptures, mosaics, pottery, arms and armour, dishes, cups and vases, caskets, reliquaries, brooches, jewellery, clocks, watches, coins, medals, prints and drawings. Made out of gold, silver, precious stones, marble and other less valuable materials, most are examples of fine craftsmanship or high art, recognised even in their own day as objects of great value. This explains why so many of them, particularly the British ones, were found in buried hordes.

Britain is particularly well represented, as one would

*British Museum*

# British Museum

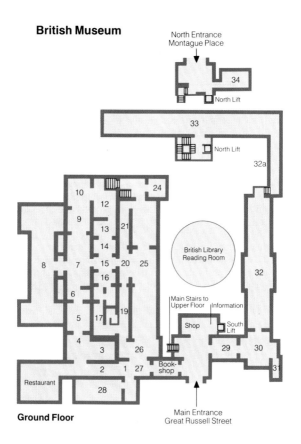

North Entrance
Montague Place

34

North Lift

33

North Lift

32a

10

12

24

9

13    21

14

8    7    15    20    25

16

6

5    17    19

4

3    26

2    1    27

28

Restaurant

British Library
Reading Room

32

Main Stairs to
Upper Floor    Information

Shop    South
Lift

29    30

31

Book-
shop

Main Entrance
Great Russell Street

## Ground Floor

1-15 Greek and Roman Antiquities
16-24, 26 Western Asian and Assyrian Antiquities
25 Egyptian Sculpture
29-32a British Library
27, 28 Temporary exhibitions
33, 34 Oriental

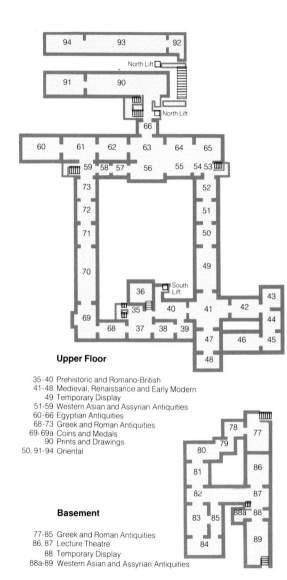

**Upper Floor**

35-40 Prehistoric and Romano-British
41-48 Medieval, Renaissance and Early Modern
49 Temporary Display
51-59 Western Asian and Assyrian Antiquities
60-66 Egyptian Antiquities
68-73 Greek and Roman Antiquities
69, 69a Coins and Medals
90 Prints and Drawings
50, 91-94 Oriental

**Basement**

77-85 Greek and Roman Antiquities
86, 87 Lecture Theatre
88 Temporary Display
88a-89 Western Asian and Assyrian Antiquities

expect. But there are also large collections covering many other civilisations and eras: prehistoric man, ancient Egypt, the Assyrian empire, Greece and Rome, Europe in the Dark Ages, the Middle Ages and the Renaissance. Then there are the galleries covering China, Japan, India and other parts of Asia.

To help you decide in advance what to see (always the best policy with a large museum), a selection of the most famous individual exhibits is listed below with their relevant room numbers:

### *Ground floor:*

8 – Elgin Marbles – 5thC BC sculptures from the Parthenon in Athens

25 – Rosetta Stone – inscribed basalt slab from ancient Egypt which led to the decipherment of Egyptian hieroglyphics

30a – Lindisfarne gospels – one of the most beautiful English illuminated manuscripts, produced at the monastery of Lindisfarne in the 7thC

30 – Magna Carta – the 1215 charter of English liberties

### *Upper floor:*

37 – Lindow Man – the corpse of a ritually-slaughtered ancient Briton preserved in a peat bog for over 2000 years

40 – Mildenhall silver treasure – a superb set of 4thC AD Roman silver tableware found in Suffolk in the 1940s

41 – Sutton Hoo treasure – Anglo-Saxon treasures from the ship burial of a 7thC East Anglian king

42 – Lewis chessmen – Scandinavian chess pieces carved from walrus tusks in the 12thC

60 – Egyptian mummies, animals and humans eerily preserved

70 – Portland vase – a beautiful blue and white glass vase made in Italy around the beginning of the Christian era, so called because it was owned by the Dukes of Portland before being bought by the Museum in 1945

---

**British Museum**
*Open 10.00-17.00 Mon-Sat, 14.30-18.00 Sun.* Admission free.
Shop. Guided tours of highlights. Guidebook. Films. Research facilities.
*Refreshments*: Excellent licensed restaurant serving hot & cold meals from a changing menu *12.00-16.15 Mon-Sat, 14.45-17.15 Sun.* Café serving drinks and snacks *10.00-16.15 Mon-Sat, 14.45-17.15 Sun.*
*Educational facilities*: Tours for schools, worksheets, lectures, workshops.
&#9855; Full access. Toilet.
&#9758; Holborn, Russell Square

## British Optical Association Foundation Collection

British College of Optometrists, 10 Knaresborough     6 B2
Place SW5. 071-373 7765.

The BOA museum came to the British College of
Optometrists when the Association was incorporated into the
College in 1980. Now displayed in one room, it contains a
fascinating collection of optical aids made over the past 400
years. There are spectacles from the 16thC, the earliest ones
without side-pieces; lorgnettes and spy-glasses from Georgian
and Regency times; early opera glasses and binoculars;
pince-nez and quizzing glasses (monocles); industrial and other
special spectacles; lenses; and early opthalmic instruments and
testing equipment. Many of the exhibits, especially the fashionable quizzing glasses and spy-glasses, are made from silver and
gold and are finely decorated with enamels and engravings.
There is also a good collection of paintings, prints, coins, china
and small sculptures, all with some optical relevance.

---

**British Optical Association Foundation Collection**
*Open by appointment only 10.00-16.00 Mon-Fri.* Admission free.
Research facilities.
&#9855; Full access
&#9854; Earl's Court

---

## Brunel's Engine House

Tunnel Road, Rotherhithe SE16. 081-318 2489.

This early Victorian engine-house was built to house the
steam engines which once drained the Thames Tunnel
between Rotherhithe and Wapping. The world's first major
underwater thoroughfare, the tunnel was built between 1825
and 1843 by the great engineer, Marc Isambard Brunel (1769-
1849), father of Isambard Kingdom Brunel (1806-1859).
Inside you can see one of the old pumping engines and an
exhibition describing how the project was bravely carried
through to completion despite terrible odds in the shape of
floods, human tragedy and financial disaster. The engine
house became redundant in 1913 when the railway line
through the tunnel was electrified. Following restoration, it
was opened as a museum in 1980.

---

**Brunel's Engine House**
*Open 12.00-16.00 first Sun of each month.* Admission charge.
Sales desk. Guided tours. Films.
*Educational facilities*: Tours for schools, lectures.
&#9855; Partial access
&#9854; Rotherhithe

---

## Cabinet War Rooms

Clive Steps, King Charles Street SW1. 071-930 6961.      4 F5

From this underground bunker near Whitehall, Churchill and his war cabinet and generals directed operations during World War II. The top leaders actually used it only during the worst of the German air raids (sometimes sleeping as well as working here), but parts, like the Map Room – the nerve centre of the whole complex, were manned continually day and night throughout the war, whatever the conditions above ground. Whenever there was an air-raid, a sign was put up saying, in a suitably understated English way, windy. You can still see this sign, along with many other evocative relics of those dark and desperate days – from maps, telephones and office furniture to files and notepads – complete with jottings – just as they were left when the rooms were closed and locked up in August 1945. When they were reopened 40 years later as little as possible was changed. The keys to all the rooms are still on hooks on the back of a door and the unplastered brick walls are still covered in their original cream paint.

*Cabinet War Rooms*

Apart from the map room, with its convoy maps, air raid charts and white, green and black telephones, the main rooms on show are the Cabinet Room, arranged as for a meeting on 15 October 1940 during the Blitz, and Churchill's bedroom-cum-office (not even prime ministers had separate bedrooms in these exceedingly cramped quarters). You can also see the tiny transatlantic telephone room (no bigger than a broom cupboard – which is actually what it was) where Churchill spoke direct to President Roosevelt. Amongst Churchill's personal possessions are his chromium-plated helmet and two bottles of his favourite champagne (Pol Roger). Over the loudspeaker you can hear some of his broadcasts and other familiar World War II sounds, from the eerie air-raid siren to wartime songs. The free audio guide with its dramatisations of cabinet meetings and primeministerial phone calls, is recommended.

---

**Cabinet War Rooms**
*Open 10.00-18.00 Mon-Sun. May close at short notice on State occasions.* Admission charge.
Shop. Guided tours. Guidebook.
*Educational facilities*: Tours for schools, worksheets, lectures, workshops, audio pack.
⑤ Full access. Toilets.
⊖ Charing Cross, Westminster

---

### Chartered Insurance Institute Museum
The Hall, 20 Aldermanbury EC2. 071-606 3835.     5 D2
The insurance business began in the late 17thC with house-owners insuring their property against fire. They put metal marks on their houses to indicate the 'office' they were insured with and relied on private fire brigades run by the various offices to attend to conflagrations. In this small one-room museum on the second floor of the Insurance Institute's building in the City you can see a fine collection of these historic fire marks dating right back to the beginnings of the industry. They are arranged in order of the establishment of each office, and then in order of issue. You can also see a small collection of firefighting and firemen's equipment, including three old hand-pumps and some glass hand grenades used for dousing fires. On the staircase between the third and fifth floors there are many more firemarks: first German ones and then another large collection of British marks.

---

**Chartered Insurance Institute Museum**
*Open 10.00-16.00 Mon-Fri.* Admission free.
&#9855; Partial access – difficult steps up to museum. Toilet.
&#8658; St Paul's

---

## Chelsea Physic Garden

66 Royal Hospital Road SW3. 071-352 5646.                6 F4

A triangular-shaped garden of 3½ acres (1.5ha) down by the river in Chelsea. Founded by the Society of Apothecaries in 1673 to grow medicinal plants, it is one of the oldest botanical gardens in Europe and the second oldest in England after Oxford. Though still very much a working research institute and plant-growing establishment, it is also a place of great beauty and charm, as many people discover when they visit during the summer months. Visitors can stroll around the herb garden, the 18thC rock garden – made with lava brought back from Iceland and old stone from the Tower of London – and the botanical order beds. And they can see the largest outdoor olive tree in Britain, 30ft (9.1m) high, and many other fine and rare trees, all thriving in this warm and protected micro-climate. As you sit on one of the many benches scattered about, the Chelsea Embankment traffic thundering by beyond the old brick wall could be another age away.

---

**Chelsea Physic Garden**
*Open mid Mar-mid Oct 14.00-17.00 Wed & Sun.* Admission charge.
Shop. Guided tours. Guidebook. Research facilities.
*Refreshments*: Tearoom serving snacks and high teas *14.00-17.00.*
*Educational facilities*: Tours for schools, worksheets, lectures, work-shops.
&#9855; Full access. Toilet.
&#8658; Sloane Square

---

## Clink Prison

1 Clink Street SE1. 071-403 6515.                5 E4

This exhibition, in the dark cellars of an old warehouse in riverside Southwark, tells in words and pictures the strange story of the Clink prison and the Liberty of the Clink. The Clink, from which we get the slang word for prison, was the private prison of the Bishops of Winchester. The area around it, which the Bishops controlled all through the Middle Ages and later, was known as the Liberty of the Clink. Despite its close connections with the Church, the Liberty developed into London's red-light district. There were stewhouses – steam-baths-cum-brothels – bear- and bull-baiting rings, and later, theatres, including Shakespeare's Globe. The Clink was filled first with prostitutes, then during the Reformation with religious dissenters, and finally in the 17thC and 18thC with debtors. Rioters burned it down in 1780.

The Exhibition claims to be on the actual site of the prison and covers not just the Clink and the Liberty, but also medieval punishments and prostitution as well. The more explicit material is displayed in an adults-only room – complete with red lights of course. A relatively new feature of the Clink is its very own resident armourer, a skilled craftsman who makes real suits of armour in his workshop inside the Exhibition. It's more than likely that your tour will be accompanied by the clank – or should it be clink – of hammer on metal as he bashes out another commission. Orders welcomed.

---

**Clink Prison**
*Open 10.00-20.00 Mon-Sun.* Admission charge.
Shop. Guided tours. Guidebook.
*Educational facilities*: Tours for schools, lectures, workshops.
🚫 Partial access
⊖ London Bridge

---

## Clockmakers' Company Collection

The Clock Room, Guildhall Library,            5 D2
Aldermanbury EC2. 071-606 3030.

This is the oldest and most comprehensive horological collection in the world. In terms of historical importance it is second only to the Ilbert collection in the British Museum. It spans 500 years from the 15thC to the 20thC though it is strongest on clocks and watches made during the life of the Clockmakers' Company. This was founded in 1631 and is one of the few City Livery Companies still actively engaged in the trade it was set up to regulate.

The collection is housed in a special room at the entrance to the Guildhall Library in the City. All is quiet save for the tick-tock and occasional chime of the dozen or so long-case clocks lining the walls. The rest of the collection is displayed in 11 glass cases, one of which contains a large set of watchkeys, fobs and châtelaines.

With its long-case, lantern and table clocks, many by famous makers such as Thomas Tompion, Edward East, Daniel Quare and George Graham, the collection covers the development of the domestic clock fairly well. But, mainly for reasons of space, it is strongest on watches. These date from the late 16thC and include such historically important instruments as the first watch to be compensated against the effects of heat and cold (1752) and the oldest surviving self-winding watch (1785). Many of the watches are beautifully engraved or chased and some are decorated with little enamel pictures.

Where the collection is unrivalled is in its watches and marine chronometers made between 1770 and 1820 when precision timekeeping was being developed. Pride of place here, and the number one position in the whole collection, goes to H5, the marine chronometer made by John Harrison to prove that his previous version, H4 (in the National Maritime Museum, see page 58) was no fluke. Harrison's invention solved the problem of longitude once and for all and, for the first time, enabled sailors to plot their exact positions at sea.

---

**Clockmakers' Company Collection**
*Open 09.30-16.45 Mon-Fri.* Admission free.
🅿 Full access. Toilet.
⊖ St Paul's

---

## Commonwealth Institute

Kensington High Street W8. 071-603 4535.                    3 B6
Founded in 1887 as the Imperial Institute, the Commonwealth Institute's job is to promote understanding between the 50 countries and 1.25 billion people who make up the modern Commonwealth. Around the distinctive 1950s hall, roofed in Zambian copper, colourful displays describe and illustrate the geography, climate, industry, wildlife, crafts, culture and history of all different member countries, associated states and dependencies. Islands and small territories from Anguilla to the Turks & Caicos are on the top level; Africa from Botswana to Zimbabwe is on the middle level; large countries such as Australia and India, and the islands of the Pacific, are on the lower level. Wide use is made of excellent dioramas and models to give three-dimensional views of different landscapes, and some displays, like Kenya's, are designed in the style of local buildings. Reggae music, croaking frogs, crickets, jungle noises and other sounds help evoke regional atmospheres, especially for Jamaica and Papua New Guinea. Exhibits range from stuffed animals, tinned foods and bales of cotton to musical instruments, basketwork, motorbikes (the TT winners from the Isle of Man), and, for New Zealand, a mechanical dairy cow with bellows for lungs. Press a button and it will breathe and emit milk! The

Bhownagree gallery shows work by contemporary Commonwealth artists.

---

**Commonwealth Institute**
*Open 10.00-17.00 Mon-Sat, 14.00-17.00 Sun.* Admission free (charge sometimes made for special exhibitions).
Bookshop. Guided tours. Guidebook. Films. Research facilities.
*Refreshments*: Licensed restaurant, serving hot & cold meals *10.00-16.45 Mon-Sat;* drinks & snacks only *14.45-16.45 Sun.*
*Educational facilities*: Tours for schools, worksheets, lectures, workshops.
🛋 Full access. Toilet.
⊖ High Street Kensington

---

## Crystal Palace Museum
Anerley Hill, Norwood SE19. 081-778 2173 (081-676 0700 *Sun afternoon*).

The Crystal Palace was the great iron and glass structure by Sir Joseph Paxton put up in Hyde Park for the Great Exhibition of 1851. When the exhibition closed it was taken down and re-erected on Sydenham Heights in south London. There it became the much-loved venue of hundreds of shows, festivals and spectacles. Fire ended its career in 1936, although the spectacularly large ruins remain. The one-room Crystal Palace Museum, run by the Crystal Palace Foundation, tells the story of the Palace through words, pictures and a small but growing collection of exhibits, such as souvenirs and programmes and excavated pieces of the original building.

---

**Crystal Palace Museum**
*Open 14.00-17.00 Sun & Bank Hols, 14.00-16.00 3rd Wed in the month.* Admission free but donations welcome.
Shop. Guided tours.
*Educational facilities*: Tours for schools.
🛋 No access
⇌ Crystal Palace

---

## Cutty Sark and Gipsy Moth IV
King William Walk, Greenwich SE10. 081-858 3445.

Built for speed and launched on the Clyde in 1869, the *Cutty Sark* spent her early years in the China tea trade. Later she switched to freighting wool from Australia. Bringing the new season's clip from Sydney to London in record time each year she earned herself the reputation of being the fastest clipper ship afloat. Now this magnificent example of sailing technology, fully rigged with her 152ft (46m) main mast soaring above the Greenwich riverside, is moored in dry dock. Below decks, several cabins can be seen, together with an exhibition chronicling the ship's history and the various trades she worked in. Down on the lowest part of the ship is the largest collection of painted ships figureheads in Britain.

Near the *Cutty Sark* and also in dry dock is the 53ft (16m) ketch, *Gipsy Moth IV*, used by Sir Francis Chichester when he became the first man to sail round the world single-handed, in 1966-67. *Open, as* Cutty Sark, *Easter-Oct only.* Admission charge. Ⓐ No access.

---

**Cutty Sark**
*Open Apr-Sep 10.00-18.00 Mon-Sat, 12.00-17.00 Sun & Good Fri; Oct-Mar 10.30-17.00 Mon-Sat, 12.00-17.00 Sun.* Admission charge.
Passport ticket provides entry to the *Cutty Sark*, National Maritime Museum, the Old Royal Observatory, and the Queen's House (all in Greenwich) but not *Gipsy Moth IV*.
Shop. Guided tours. Guidebook.
*Educational facilities*: Tours for schools, worksheets, lectures.
Ⓐ Partial access
⇻ Greenwich

---

## Design Centre

28 Haymarket SW1. 071-839 8000.                              4 E3

This is the public face of the government-sponsored Design Council, which promotes the use of good design in British industry. The main display area on the ground floor is the scene for regular exhibitions demonstrating the role design can play in the British economy. Here you can see everything from domestic pieces such as cutlery and furniture to construction fittings for buildings. Upstairs in the Young Designers Centre, design work by young people in all disciplines is exposed to public scrutiny. Like the Design Museum in Butler's Wharf, the Design Centre is especially interesting for showing how good design can make even everyday objects visually fresh and interesting.

---

**Design Centre**
*Open 10.00-18.00 Mon-Sat, 13.00-18.00 Sun.* Admission free.
Bookshop. Guided tours. Films.
*Educational facilities*: Tours for schools, worksheets, lectures, work-shops, activity centre.
Ⓐ Partial access – ground floor only.
⊖ Piccadilly Circus

## Design Museum

Butler's Wharf, Shad Thames SE1. 071-407 6261.          5 G4
Opened in 1987, the Design Museum was the inspiration of Sir Terence Conran, the man who put design into ordinary British homes through the Habitat range of products. It is housed in a modern riverside building on the South Bank, downstream from Tower Bridge.

The second floor, with its large windows overlooking the Thames, is the museum's main 'permanent' display area. Permanent is in inverted commas because nothing is absolutely fixed here. The large, light space is divided into two sections. In what is called the *Collection* you can see generations of everyday objects side by side, showing how design has changed their appearance, and sometimes the way they are used as well. Overall, this section illustrates the development of design in mass production, and explains what factors – commercial, social, aesthetic, technological, functional – designers have to take into account in their work. The objects on show could be anything from tableware, telephones, radios or chairs to desklamps, hoovers, typewriters and office furniture. You might also see bicycles and cars.

Behind the *Collection* is the *Review* section. This is a display of concepts, prototypes and new products – in some cases so new that they are not yet on the market. The beauty of this section is that it allows you to compare what designers are doing today with what their predecessors did in the past (as seen in the *Collection*). The other interesting aspect of the *Review* is that it shows some products which will never be launched in the UK. Sometimes they look so much better than the things we have that you can't help wondering why they are never marketed here.

In the library section right at the back of this floor you can browse through design magazines, find out more about the exhibits via computer terminals, play interactive video design games, and watch videos of designers talking about their work.

---

**Design Museum**
*Open 11.30-18.30 Tue-Sun & Bank Hols.* Admission charge.
Shop. Films. Research facilities.
*Refreshments*: Blueprint Café, licensed, serving hot & cold meals from outstanding Modern European menu *11.30-18.30 Tue-Sun.*
*Educational facilites*: Tours for schools, worksheets, lectures, workshops, video displays.
&#9855; Full access. Toilet.
&#9961; London Bridge

---

## Fan Museum

12 Crooms Hill, Greenwich SE10. 081-858 7879.

Two 18thC terraced houses in Greenwich have been immaculately restored to form the world's first, and so far only, fan museum. It opened in 1991. The museum's collection is particularly strong in European fans of the 18thC and 19thC and is based mainly on the 2000 and more examples collected by the museum's founder and honorary curator, Hélène Alexander.

The ground floor displays cover the art, craft and history of fans – how they were (and are) made, the various types such as fixed, folding and articulate, and the materials used (ivory and tortoise-shell as well as paper and textiles). Upstairs, changing exhibitions look more closely at the subjects which have inspired fanmakers and decorators since fans became fashionable in Europe in the 17thC. Two of the finest fans in the collection are the jewelled fan made in Germany for the Queen of Romania in the 1880s, and the mother of pearl fan used by George V's mother-in-law, the Duchess of Teck. Some of the more lighthearted examples include fans made in the shape of butterflies, birds, cats and dogs.

In the basement workshops, the museum carries on the fan-making tradition by creating new fans and restoring old ones.

---

**Fan Museum**

*Open 11.00-16.30 Tue-Sat, 12.00-16.30 Sun.* Admission charge (free to OAPs and disabled *14.00-16.30 Tue*).

Shop. Guided tours. Guidebook. Research facilities.

*Educational facilities*: Tours for schools, lectures, fan-making classes by appointment.

&#x267F; Full access

&#x2762; Greenwich

---

## Florence Nightingale Museum

2 Lambeth Palace Road SE1. 071-620 0374.          4 G6

An award-winning museum devoted to the life and work of 'the lady with the lamp', Florence Nightingale. Created in 1989 within the very hospital (St Thomas's) where she founded the first-ever school of nursing over 100 years ago, the museum contains many of her personal possessions, including one of her famous lamps. There are also several reconstructed room sets: a ward in the Crimea (where she made her name); the sitting room of her home, and a Victorian slum cottage of the kind common during her lifetime. These, plus an excellent

20-minute audio-visual on the history of nursing, midwifery and hospital work generally, help put Florence's life and labours in their proper historical context.

---

**Florence Nightingale Museum**
*Open 10.00-16.00 Tue-Sun & Bank Hols.* Admission charge.
Shop.
*Educational facilities*: Tours for schools. Lectures. Workshops.
&#9855; Full access. Toilet.
&#9229; Westminster, Waterloo

---

## Geffrye Museum

Kingsland Road, Hackney E2. 071-739 9893.
Consisting entirely of re-created room interiors (mainly sitting rooms), the Geffrye Museum shows the changing styles of furniture and decoration used in town houses from Tudor times to the 1950s. With one exception, the rooms are laid out in a straight line along the ground floor of an old almshouse built in 1715 with money left by Sir Robert Geffrye, Lord Mayor of London and Master of the Ironmongers' Company. Early this century the almshouse was acquired by the London County Council and opened in 1914 as a museum of furniture and domestic interiors. Furniture- and cabinet-making had long been traditional industries in the Kingsland Road area.

Apart from some carpets and curtains, all the exhibits in the museum – panelling, chimneypieces, furniture, musical instruments, pictures, clocks, mirrors, candlesticks, knick-

*Geffrye Museum*

knacks – are original, though the room settings are artificial. Until the 20thC they tend to represent the more well-to-do homes; poorer homes have not survived.

There are ten main rooms altogether: Tudor, Stuart, William and Mary, early and late Georgian, Regency, Victorian, Arts and Crafts, 1930s and (upstairs over the exhibition area) the 1950s. As you pass through, it is fascinating to see at a glance how interiors became lighter and more refined up to the 18thC, then began to grow heavy and cluttered in the 19thC, before becoming lighter, but also cheaper, in the mass-production utility era of the mid-20thC.

As well as the main rooms, you can also see the former chapel of the almshouse, a 'Cabinet of Curiosities', three 18thC shop fronts, and a small open-hearth kitchen full of cooking equipment used in the 18thC and 19thC.

---

**Geffrye Museum**
*Open 10.00-17.00 Tue-Sat, 14.00-17.00 Sun & Bank Hols.*
Admission free.
Shop. Guided tours. Guidebook. Research facilities.
*Refreshments:* Coffee shop *10.30-16.30.*
*Educational facilities:* Tours for schools, workshops.
⟨&⟩ Almost full access – one room only inaccessible. Toilet.
⊖ Liverpool Street (then bus 22, 22b, 48, 67, 149, 243 or 243a)

---

## Guards' Museum
Wellington Barracks, Birdcage Walk SW1.                    4 D5
071-930 4466 x 3271.

Opened in 1988 in a special room beneath the barracks parade ground, the Guards' Museum tells the story of the five infantry regiments that make up the famous Guards division. You start over 300 years ago at the time of the Civil War when the three oldest Guards regiments – Coldstream, Grenadier and Scots Guards – were formed. Then, moving through the 18thC and 19thC, you come to the South African Wars when the Irish Guards were formed, followed by the First World War when the Welsh Guards were founded. The latest display covers the Falklands War.

Exhibits on show include historic uniforms and bearskins; weapons from pikes and swords to machine guns and grenades; personal possessions such as soldiers' notebooks, an officer's travelling canteen from the Peninsular Wars, and a surgeon's kit from the Crimea; Dervish, German and Argentinian war trophies; relics of three great Guards generals

– Marlborough, Wellington and Lord Alexander of Tunis; and finally, regimental curiosities such as an old punishment book, fearsome cat o' nine tails, and the lock from Hougoumont Farm (a key position defended by the Guards at Waterloo).

Outside the museum the Buckingham Palace guard forms up each morning before marching off to take part in the Changing of the Guard ceremony. Timing your visit to coincide with the ceremony (*daily at 11.30 in summer; every other day in winter* – details in national press) will definitely add to your tour of the museum.

---

**Guards' Museum**
*Open 10.00-16.00 Sat-Thur. Closed some ceremonial days.*
Admission charge.
Shop. Guided tours. Guidebooks. Research facilities.
*Educational facilities*: Tours for schools.
&#91;&#8255;&#93; Partial access. Toilet.
&#1012; St James's Park

---

### Hahnemann Relics

Hahnemann House, 2 Powis Place,          2 B5
Great Ormond Street WC1. 071-837 9469.
Hahnemann House, close to the Royal London Homeopathic Hospital, is a postgraduate training centre for doctors wanting to develop their knowledge of homeopathic medicine. In one of the lecture rooms there are four display cases containing letters, seals, pictures, original remedies and other personal possessions belonging to Dr Samuel Hahnemann (1755-1843), the founder of homeopathy. The house, one of many 18thC buildings in the area, was given to one of Hahnemann's early disciples in the last century.

---

**Hahnemann Relics**
*Open by appointment only 10.00-17.00 Mon-Fri.* Admission free.
&#91;&#8255;&#93; Full access
&#1012; Russell Square

---

### Harrow School Old Speech Room Gallery

Church Hill, Harrow-on-the-Hill, Middlesex. 081-869 1205/081-422 2196.
Harrow is well-enough-known as a public school, but few realise that it also has a large and important museum and art collection built up mainly through the gifts of old boys over the past 150 years. A selection, including many of the best pieces, is on display in the school's modern gallery, created in

the 1970s out of the old debating chamber or speech room. On show are splendid Egyptian, Greek and Etruscan antiquities from the Sir John Gardner Wilkinson collection; English watercolours, including works by Cotman and Turner; modern British paintings and etchings; a natural history collection with some beautiful coloured butterflies from New Guinea; printed books and general school memorabilia. Occasional exhibitions show items associated with famous old boys, notably Byron and Churchill.

---

**Harrow School Old Speech Room Gallery**
*Open termtime 14.30-17.00 Mon-Tue & Thur-Sun; closed some exeat weekends. Holidays 14.30-17.00 Mon-Fri.* Admission free. Shop. Guided tours. Guidebook.
&#9855; No access
&#9758; Harrow-on-the-Hill

---

### HMS Belfast
Morgan's Lane, Tooley Street SE1. 071-407 6434.    5 F4
Launched shortly before World War II, the 11,000 ton cruiser HMS *Belfast* played a key role in the sinking of the

HMS *Belfast*

*Scharnhorst* and last fired her guns in anger in the Korean War. Saved from the scrapyard in the 1960s, she was opened as a floating museum on the Thames in 1971. The last survivor of the Navy's fleet of big-gun ships, she is a powerfully atmospheric relic of naval warfare before the electronic age.

A clearly marked route allows you to explore all seven decks of the ship. Among other things, you will see the bridge, operations and communications rooms, 6-inch gun turrets, the engine room and boiler room, galley, mess decks old and new, chapel, laundry, punishment cells and sickbay. Special displays provide more information about the history of the *Belfast* herself and some of the naval operations in which she took part, including D-Day. They also cover more general subjects, such as the development of cruisers and battleships since the 19thC; gunnery and mine-laying; and the Navy today, including the Fleet Air Arm, the Royal Marines and the Royal Ulster Rifles.

---

**HMS Belfast**
*Open Mar-Oct 10.00-17.20 (to 16.00 Nov-Mar) Mon-Sun.* Admission charge.
Shop. Guided tours. Guidebook. Films.
*Refreshments*: Café serving hot & cold snacks and light meals *10.00-16.30 Mar-Oct, 11.30-15.30 Nov-Mar.*
*Educational facilities*: Tours for schools, worksheets, lectures, workshops.
🚹 Partial access. Toilet.
⊖ London Bridge, Tower Hill

---

## Horniman Museum

100 London Road, Forest Hill SE23. 081-699 1872.
The Horniman Museum is very much the creation of one man. That man was Frederick Horniman MP, tea merchant and fanatical collector. It was he who established the amazing ethnographical, musical and natural history collections for which the Horniman is famous; and it was he who gave the collections, along with their museum building, to the people of London in 1901.

In the Ethnographical Hall you will see all kinds of wonderful things illustrating the way of life, customs and beliefs, and arts and crafts of indigenous peoples and country folk from all over the world, including Britain and Europe. Besides a large collection of masks from many countries, there are wood carvings from Africa, a mummy from ancient Egypt, Indian clothes from North America, and Buddha statues from Burma. And from Britain? Farm tools from Huntingdonshire.

In the second hall, the world-class musical instrument collection contains over 6000 examples with row upon row of familiar instruments like clarinets, flutes and trombones, as well as strange and exotic instruments like Bulgarian bag pipes, Kenyan trumpets and Mongolian spike fiddles. Representing most countries in the world and dating from as early as 1400 BC, they are interestingly arranged according to the way they produce sound, for example by resonance, plucking or blowing.

The natural history collection fills most of the second hall and contains case after case of fossils, shells, stuffed birds and small animals, and the bones of larger ones, including, in the Evolution section, a human skeleton. The centrepiece is a huge stuffed walrus procured by Horniman from Hudson Bay. Children can step on some scales and compare their weight with that of the poor long-dead creature. It has to be said that, apart from the excellent Living Waters Aquarium, these scales are about the most modern thing in the museum. On the other hand, although its presentation may be a bit old-fashioned, it does all it can to avoid being academic and has a light-hearted atmosphere much enjoyed by children.

---

**Horniman Museum**
*Open 10.30-17.50 Mon-Sat, 14.00-17.50 Sun.* Admission free.
Shop. Guided tours. Guidebooks. Films. Research facilities.
*Refreshments:* Café serving hot & cold meals and snacks *11.30-16.30 Mon-Sat, to 17.30 Sun.*
*Educational facilities:* Tours for schools, worksheets, lectures, work-shops.
&#9855; Full access. Toilet.
&#8812; Forest Hill

---

## Imperial War Museum

Lambeth Road SE1. 071-416 5000.                              5 B6

Formed in the aftermath of the First World War, the Imperial War Museum's brief is to record *all* British military operations since 1914. But although its building (the old Bethlem lunatic asylum, built in 1815) has recently been redeveloped to make it one of the most modern and stylish museums in London, it still only has room for the First and Second World Wars. New space is planned for later conflicts.

The museum is divided up into three main areas: large exhibits; historical displays; and a collection of war art. Most of the large exhibits are in the all-white, glass-roofed central hall which you come to on first entering the museum. Around the red London bus used on the Western Front stand tanks, jeeps, guns, mini-subs, and a V2 rocket. Suspended from the ceiling are a V1 doodlebug and various fighter planes, including a Sopwith Camel biplane, a Spitfire and a Mustang from the Second World War.

The planes are best viewed from the two viewing balconies. The first balcony also has its own large exhibits, notably the cockpits from two bombers: a Lancaster and a Halifax. You can walk through the latter and see how cramped these fragile-looking aircraft were inside. The upper viewing balcony gives on to the museum's two main art galleries, one for each of the world wars. Among many fine and moving paintings, reliefs and sculptures, keep an eye out particularly for the menacing black head of Mussolini by Bertelli, just inside the Second World War Gallery.

The superb chronological and subject displays in the basement area relate mainly to the First and Second World Wars, but a smaller section in the middle covers the important interwar years and the rise of Fascism. The glass-fronted display cases contain a mass of fascinating material, culled from the home front as well as the front line. To bring out the human experience of war, both military and civilian, handsets allow you to listen to recordings of wartime experiences, while screens show original films, some with modern commentaries. Each main war sequence also has an 'experience'. For the First World War it's a walk-through re-creation of a front-line trench on the Somme in 1916. For the Second World War it's the Blitz in London (there is an extra charge for this). Both have special lighting, sound and smell effects and the latter shudders as the bombs crump down. You really wish that cup of tea proffered at the end of the 'experience' was real!

---

**Imperial War Museum**
*Open 10.00-18.00 Mon-Sun.* Admission charge (except *Fri*).
Shop. Guided tours. Guidebook. Films. Research facilities.
*Refreshments*: Licensed restaurant serving fresh home-made dishes *12.00-14.30 Mon-Sun.*
*Educational facilities*: Tours for schools, worksheets, lectures.
&#9855; Full access. Toilet.
&#9711; Lambeth North

## Jewel Tower

Old Palace Yard, Abingdon Street W1. 071-222 2219.    4 F6
This L-shaped tower across the road from the Houses of
Parliament is the only surviving part of the medieval Palace of
Westminster, built in 1365 to house the monarch's personal
jewels and valuables. Later it was used to store the records of
the House of Lords and then, from 1869-1938, it was the
Weights and Measures Testing Department of the Board
of Trade. Some of the Department's historic weights and
measures are on show in one of the tower's six bare rooms
(these are on three floors, linked by a narrow stone spiral
staircase). In other rooms there are maps and pictures
illustrating the history of old Westminster, unused designs
submitted for the new Houses of Parliament (rebuilt after the
disastrous fire of 1834), and various bowls, bottles and other
artefacts excavated over the years from the tower's moat and
other places nearby. Chief among these is the 1200-year-old
Westminster sword. A large permanent exhibition on the
history of Parliament is due to open in the tower sometime in
1992.

> **Jewel Tower**
> *Open Apr-Sep 10.00-13.00 & 14.00-18.00 Mon-Sun, Oct-Mar 10.00-*
> *13.00 & 14.00-16.00 Tue-Sun.* Admission charge.
> Shop. Guidebook.
> &#x267F; No access
> &#x229D; Westminster

## Jewish Museum

Woburn House, Tavistock Square WC1. 071-388 4525.    1 F5
Part of a Jewish communal centre opened in 1932, this small,
one-room museum contains a varied and fascinating collection of ritual art and antiques illustrating Jewish life, history
and religion, mainly in Britain. Although there are one or two
objects from antiquity and medieval England, the main part of
the collection consists of 18thC ritual objects – often in fine
embroidery or silver – from City of London synagogues:
scrolls, sabbath lamps, Torah mantles, bells, rings, plates and
mugs, illuminated marriage contracts and many other fine and
rare things. The centrepiece of the collection is a massive
16thC Venetian Ark of the Law, rescued from a servant's
bedroom in a Northumberland castle where it was being used
as a wardrobe.

> **Jewish Museum**
> *Open 10.00-16.00 Tue-Fri, (to 12.45 Fri in winter), 10.00-12.45 Sun.*
> *Closed Jewish Hols.* Admission free.
> Shop. Guided tours. Research facilities.
> *Educational facilities*: Tours for schools, worksheets, lectures.
> 🅔 Full access
> ⊖ Euston Square, Euston

## Kathleen & May

St Mary Overy Dock, Cathedral Street SE1.      5 E4
071-403 3965.

The *Kathleen & May* is the last of the hundreds of three-masted topsail schooners which not so long ago dominated the coastal trade around Britain's shores. Since 1986 she has been open to visitors in a small wet dock off the Thames near Southwark Cathedral. The ship can be explored, and below decks you can see an exhibition covering coastal trade and the history of the ship, which was built in 1900 on the River Dee near Chester.

> **Kathleen & May**
> *Open 10.00-17.00 Mon-Sun.* Admission charge.
> Shop. Guidebook. Lectures.
> 🅔 No access
> ⊖ London Bridge

## Kew Bridge Steam Museum

Green Dragon Lane, Brentford, Middlesex. 081-568 4757.
Visiting this museum is a bit like visiting a factory, which is perhaps not so surprising since not so long ago it was a working pumping station and a vital part of London's water supply network. Water came from the Thames via filter beds at Hampton. It was then pumped several miles to reservoirs in Kensington, west London, and from there fed into the mains and private homes.

    The engines used to send the water that great distance were huge steam engines housed in massive cathedral-like engine-houses. Five such engines were installed at Kew, the first in 1838. The fantastic thing about the museum is that three of them, including the oldest (dating from 1820) and the second-largest (a Cornish 90-incher) have been fully restored and can be seen pumping away at weekends when the steam is up. You can get right up close and see them from every angle because there are floor areas at both cylinder and beam level, the latter perhaps 50ft (15m) above the ground. They really are *huge* machines, and this is the largest collection of them you will see anywhere in the world. You can also see inside the rusted guts of one of the unrestored engines and get a good idea of the amount of work involved in getting just one of them going again.

The museum also has other, smaller steam engines which together with a display on the fascinating history of London's water supply are all housed in the Steam Hall, a large room warmed by the hot steam and filled with the rhythmic clackety-clack of the different engines. Outside there are diesel engines in the Diesel House, and (*during the last weekend of each month from March to November*), rides on the small industrial railway. Plans for the future include an Electric Pump House.

---

**Kew Bridge Steam Museum**
*Open 11.00-17.00 Mon-Sun (steam up at weekends & Bank Hols).*
Admission charge.
Bookshop. Guided tours. Guidebook. Films. Research facilities.
*Refreshments*: Tearoom serving snacks and cakes *11.00-17.00 Sat & Sun.*
*Educational facilities*: Tours for schools, worksheets, lectures, workshops.
&#x267F; Partial access
&#x2296; Gunnersbury (then bus 237)

---

### Livesey Museum
682 Old Kent Road, Peckham SE15. 071-639 5604.
The Livesey is a popular science and history museum, but

*South African objects made from 'rubbish', Livesey Museum*

instead of having its own permanent collection, it borrows things from other museums to create its exhibitions. Recent subjects have included Robots, Dinosaurs, the Science of Light, a History of Street Markets, and Rubbish. The exhibitions are mainly aimed at children, and the Livesey has a good reputation for putting on shows that manage to be educational and entertaining at the same time.

---

**Livesey Museum**
*Open during exhibitions 10.00-17.00 Mon-Sat.* Admission free.
Shop. Films.
*Educational facilities*: Tours for schools, worksheets, lectures, workshops.
&#9855; Partial access. Toilet.
Bus  53, 177 or 141 from central London

---

## London Dungeon

28-34 Tooley Street SE1. 071-403 0606.                          5 E4

Set in huge dark vaults beneath London Bridge station, the London Dungeon recreates the darker side of life in times gone by when execution, torture, witchcraft, superstition, plague, disease and medical remedies (every bit as horrible as the conditions they were intended to treat) were everyday facts of life.

Backed up by sophisticated technology, eerie sound effects and dramatic lighting, a series of tableaux bring to life scenes involving real historical characters, from kings and queens like Richard the Lionheart and Anne Boleyn to religious martyrs and common criminals; all victims of some particularly gruesome death, execution, torture or sheer wanton cruelty.

Special areas feature the Great Fire of London in 1666 and the guillotine of the French Revolution. Although not a museum in the strictest sense of the word, and definitely not for the squeamish, the presentations are based on historical fact and you can learn something useful, albeit of a side of life which you might rather forget!

---

**London Dungeon**
*Open Apr-Sep 10.00-17.30 Mon-Sun, Oct-Mar 10.00-16.30 Mon-Sun.* Admission charge.
Shop. Guided tours. Guidebook.
*Refreshments*: Café serving drinks and snacks.
*Educational facilities*: Tours for schools, worksheets.
&#9855; Full access. Toilets.
&#8710; London Bridge

## London Fire Brigade Museum

Winchester House, 94a Southwark Bridge Road SE1.      5 D5
071-587 4273.

Housed in the former home of Sir Eyre Massey Shaw, a
famous 19thC superintendent of the fire brigade, this little-
known museum covers the fascinating history of firefighting
in the capital over three centuries from the Great Fire of 1666
to the demise of the London County Council in 1965.

The main rooms show how the fire service developed in the
18thC through competing brigades operated by different
insurance companies, and how these came together in 1833 to
form the first London Fire Engine Establishment. One room
has been made to look like a 'gear (ie uniform) room' in a
Victorian fire station. Another focuses in more detail on the
heroic work performed by the fire brigade during the dark
days of the Blitz in World War II.

Downstairs on the ground floor the Large Appliance Room
contains the bigger exhibits: manual pumps from the early
18thC; steam pumps from the 19thC; and horse-drawn fire
engines used up to the 1920s. Outside, in the yard used by
recruits from the adjacent fire-training school, you should be
able to see some of the very latest in fire-fighting equipment.

---

**London Fire Brigade Museum**
*Guided tours by arrangement.* Admission free.
&#9855; No access
&#9758; Borough

---

## London Gas Museum

North Thames Gas, Twelvetrees Crescent, Bromley-by-Bow
E3. 071-987 2000 x 3344.

This private museum is run by British Gas on one of its opera-
tional sites in east London. Housed in a two-storey building
once used by the station engineer, it was opened in 1983 and
is very modern and up-to-date, with interesting displays and
several sets to help put things into physical context.

The ground floor covers the development of the gas
industry from its beginnings in the early 19thC to the advent
of natural gas in the late 1960s, particularly in London. The
first displays look at some of the early pioneers of the industry,
notably Frederick Winsor, founder of the Gas, Light and Coke
Company in 1812, and how town gas was manufactured and
distributed. The highlight here is an excellent tape and slide
show on the Beckton gas plant, opened in 1870 and, in its
day, the largest in the world.

Upstairs takes a closer look at the Gas, Light and Coke Company, at the people who ran it and worked for it, and at some of its most prominent customers – Buckingham Palace for example, where gas light was first installed in 1837. Here also is the museum's main collection of gas artefacts: cases full of lamps and meters, and rows of gas fires, water heaters, cookers and fridges. There is even a gas-powered radio. Realistic full-size figures show a lamplighter going about his business, a fat man getting into a hot bath with his water heater close by, and an Edwardian lady in her drawing room with its new gas fire. What a change it must have made from coal and candles!

---

**London Gas Museum**
*Open by appointment 09.30-16.00 Mon-Fri*. Admission free.
Shop. Guided tours.
*Educational facilities*: Tours for schools, worksheets, lectures, workshops.
⚑ No access
⊖ Bromley-by-Bow

---

## London Museum of Jewish Life

Sternberg Centre, 80 East End Road, Finchley N3. 081-346 2288.
This is a fairly new venture whose ultimate goal is to chronicle the social and cultural history of London's Jewish population from readmission into England during the Commonwealth in 1656 to the present day. Housed at the moment in the Sternberg Centre for Judaism, it features a permanent exhibition on the history of Jewish immigration and settlement in London, with reconstructions of a tailoring workshop, an immigrant home and an East End bakery.

---

**London Museum of Jewish Life**
*Open 10.30-17.00 Mon-Thur, 10.30-16.30 Sun (closed Jewish Hols, Bank Hols and Sun in Aug)*. Admission free.
Shop. Guided tours. Research facilities.
*Refreshments*: Café serving snacks and light lunches *11.00-14.00 Mon-Thur & Sun*.
*Educational facilities*: Tours for schools, worksheets, lectures, workshops.
⚑ Partial access. Toilet.
⊖ Finchley Central

---

## London Toy and Model Museum

21 Craven Hill W2. 071-262 7905. 3 D3
Opened in 1982, the London Toy and Model Museum has

already established itself as one of the finest toy museums in the world. An added attraction is that it doesn't compete directly with London's other main toy museum, the Bethnal Green Museum of Childhood (see page 11). Bethnal Green is strong on dolls, dolls' houses and non-mechanical toys. The London Toy and Model Museum sensibly focuses on mechanical toys, especially model railways. Together, the combined collections of the two museums – plus, of course, Pollock's Toy Museum (see page 72) – mean that nowhere else in the world can you see a larger, finer or more comprehensive collection of historic toys.

So much for the serious side. The London Toy and Model Museum is also great fun, especially for children. In the large garden at the back they can take rides on a miniature railway (steam-driven at weekends, battery-powered during the week), ride on a vintage roundabout, play on an old double-decker bus or watch $2^1/_2$, 1 and 0 gauge model railways. On the last Sunday of each month, they can bring their own trains to run on the museum's outdoor tracks, and at any time their own (non-petrol) boats to sail on the garden pond. Meanwhile, parents can take a well-earned rest in the café, positioned to command a good view of the garden. Regular events at the museum include a Model Boat Regatta in June and Teddy Bears' picnic in July.

Inside, the main collections are displayed on two floors of a pair of Victorian houses. The recommended route takes you through the shop and café and downstairs to the special exhibitions gallery. Here you start a wonderful journey through a children's world of dolls and dolls' houses, early wooden toys, Dinky cars and other miniature vehicles. Reconstructed Meccano and Basset-Lowke railway shops, animal toys and teddy bears, racing cars, aeroplanes, a typical Victorian nursery, Paddington Bear, model soldiers, penny toys, tin toys, model fire engines, and finally, the stars of the museum's collection, the model trains.

---

**London Toy & Model Museum**
*Open 10.00-17.30 Tue-Sat, 11.00-17.30 Sun.* Admission charge. Shop. Guided tours. Guidebook.
*Refreshments*: Café serving snacks *10.00-16.30 Mon-Fri, to 17.30 Sat & Sun.*
*Educational facilities*: Tours for schools.
🚫 No access
⊖ Lancaster Gate

**London Transport Museum**
Covent Garden WC2. 071-379 6344.                    4 G3
London Transport had a stroke of luck when they discovered
the old flower market in Covent Garden for their museum.
Well lit from above, and with acres of open space, it's an ideal
place in which to display their large collection of historic
public transport vehicles. Spanning well over 100 years, it
includes a complete range of buses from the horse-drawn
omnibuses of the 1870s to the modern driver-operated
Fleetliners; trams and trolleybuses; underground steam
engines and carriages and, of course some early tube trains.
There is also a 1920s reconstruction of a Shillibeer horse-
drawn omnibus, first introduced in 1829 and the forerunner of
London's modern public transport network. Underground railways followed in 1863; horse-drawn trams in 1870 and the
electric tube in 1890. Motorbuses arrived in 1899.

Generally, these immaculately maintained vehicles with their
smart livery, glossy paintwork and polished metal are, for
obvious reasons, out of bounds. But children especially will be
pleased to hear that this rule does not apply everywhere. You
can, for example, climb aboard a big red bus and operate the
controls, or enter the darkened cab of a tube train and take a
simulated journey round the Circle Line. Elsewhere there are
lots of buttons to press and various interactive video points.

For those with a more serious interest in the history of
London's public transport, there are excellent displays around
the walls telling the complete story through words and
pictures, maps and models. Films and further displays look
more closely at particular aspects and themes of the story, for
example at the City and South London Railway (the first tube),
and at the creation of London Transport in 1933. One of the
most interesting highlights London Transport's concentration
on good design in everything from station architecture to poster
graphics, and shows in particular how the modern tube map
was created. Examples of London Transport's deservedly
famous, and for older visitors, nostalgic, posters can be seen
colourfully decorating the walls all over the museum.

---

**London Transport Museum**
*Open 10.00-18.00 Mon-Sun.* Admission charge.
Shop. Guided tours. Guidebooks. Films. Research facilities.
*Educational facilities*: Tours for schools, worksheets, lectures.
🅐 Full access. Toilet.
⊖ Covent Garden

## Madame Tussaud's

Marylebone Road NW1. 071-935 6861. 1 C5

Marie Tussaud (1761-1850) brought her collection of wax portraits to England in 1802 and spent 33 years touring with it before settling permanently in London. Since then the exhibition has won worldwide fame and become one of Britain's most popular tourist attractions – something the queues outside make all too obvious.

Today the models are displayed in themed areas. The centrepiece is the Grand Hall, a large, opulently furnished room peopled with famous figures, mostly 19thC and 20thC, from Mozart and the Duke of Wellington to Yasser Arafat and Nelson Mandela. Henry VIII stands at one end of the room with all of his six wives. The current Royal Family stand facing him from the other end. They are all excellent portraits with the exception of the Prince and Princess of Wales who, for some reason, are rather off beam. It's nice to see a touch of humour with the Chelsea Pensioner and an exhausted

*Luciano Pavarotti with his figure at Madame Tussaud's*

tourist sitting on sofas which are otherwise for visitors to use. Here and in the 'Garden Party', where Dudley Moore plays the piano, Arthur Scargill sups a pint and Benny Hill acts as a commissionaire, you mingle with the figures in a way that can be slightly unnerving if you don't realise it's a model you're standing next to. Also if you sit very still on one of the sofas you find children coming up to you wide-eyed, wondering if you are real!

The most famous area is the Chamber of Horrors, a dark, dungeon-like rogues gallery showing not only famous murderers like John Christie in his squalid kitchen at 10 Rillington Place, but also means of execution such as the electric chair, the garotte and the guillotine. Mounted on the wall near the latter is the very blade which severed the head of Queen Marie Antoinette in 1793. This is one of several relics of the French Revolution in the exhibition – Marie Tussaud was actually employed at that time to take death masks from the victims of Louis XIV's Reign of Terror.

Perhaps the most unusual and interesting display is the one called 200 Years. This takes a look at both the past and future of Madame Tussaud's, and features historical documents, Tussaud memorabilia and a portrait of Madame herself, going about her grisly death mask business. It shows the oldest model in the collection (Madame du Barry, made in 1765 by Madame Tussaud's uncle and teacher) and the inner workings of the animatronic models of the future. These will be able, by means of robotics, to walk and talk.

---

**Madame Tussaud's**
*Open 10.00-17.30 Mon-Sun. Doors open earlier in summer.*
Admission charge (children under 5 years free).
Shop. Guidebook.
*Refreshments*: Restaurant serving hot & cold meals.
*Educational facilities*: Tours for schools, worksheets.
&#9855; Partial access – advance notice of visit required. Toilet.
&#10134; Baker Street

---

## Markfield Beam Engine and Museum

Markfield Road, South Tottenham N15. 081-800 7061 or (076 387) 331.
The one exhibit in this small but fascinating industrial museum is a massive, original compound beam engine powered by steam. Installed in 1886, it pumped up to 4 million gallons of north London sewage a day before being shut down finally in the 1960s. After some years of neglect a

specially-formed charity restored the noble machine to full working order and opened it to the public. Now it can be seen in action once again, driving its original pumps just as it did 100 years ago. A small exhibition alongside illustrates the vital role played by steam engines like the Markfield in public health engineering works in the 19thC and 20thC.

---

**Markfield Beam Engine and Museum**
*Open Apr-Oct occasional Sun afternoons. Phone for exact dates and times.* Admission charge.
Guided tours. Guidebook.
*Educational facilities*: Tours for schools.
&#x267F; Full access. Toilet.
&#x2296; Seven Sisters

---

## Martinware Pottery Collection

Public Library, 9-11 Osterley Park Road, Southall, Middlesex. 081-574 3412.

Here at Southall Library, a small first-floor room off the reference library has been set aside for a collection of Martinware made by the first English studio potters, the Martin brothers, at their Southall pottery between 1877 and 1923. Most of the 400 or so pieces are on loan from local people whose forebears were early customers of the four brothers. There are five display cases altogether, containing a wide variety of large and small pieces with the emphasis on decorative and household items: grotesques, toby jugs, pepper pots, vases, teapots, plates, owls and wall plaques. A Council-owned collection of Martinware clockcases can be viewed by appointment. There is also a collection of Martinware pottery at the Pitshanger Manor Museum (see page 130).

---

**Martinware Pottery Collection**
*Open 09.00-17.30 Tue, Thur & Fri; 09.00-17.00 Wed & Sat.*
Admission free.
&#x267F; No access
&#x21A8; Southall

---

## MCC Museum

Lord's Ground, St John's Wood NW8. 071-266 3825 (tours only).

Lord's, home of the Marylebone Cricket Club and named after its 18thC founder, Thomas Lord, is both the spiritual home of cricket and a private club. The MCC museum, within the club, is an integral part of a guided tour which also takes in the famous Long Room, with its old cricketing paintings, portraits of the great names of the game and display of cricket bats; the real tennis court; the new Mound stand; and the indoor practice school, with its 100 mph bowling machine. In the museum, the history of cricket is brought to life as cricket commentator Brian Johnston conducts an imaginary interview with W.G. Grace and a video shows highlights from some of the great cricketing performances captured on film. Not to be missed amongst all the historic cricketing memorabilia is the urn containing the hallowed Ashes.

---

**MCC Museum**
*Guided tours (book in advance) at 10.00, 12.00, 14.00 & 16.00 (subject to variation) Mon-Sat; 14.00 & 16.00 Sun. No tours during Test Matches, Cup Finals and preparation days.* Admission charge.
Shop. Guidebook. Research facilities.
*Educational facilities*: Tours for schools.
⟨&⟩ Partial access
⊖ St John's Wood

---

## Michael Faraday Museum

Royal Institution of Great Britain, 21 Albemarle Street W1. 071-409 2992.    4 D3

A small museum devoted to the life and work of Michael Faraday (1791-1867), the great scientist and pioneering chemist whose discoveries in electromagnetic induction laid the foundations of today's electrical industries. The museum contains a unique collection of original apparatus used by Faraday in his various experiments, plus his notebooks and personal possessions like his slide-rule and inkstand. Next to the museum room, behind a glass wall, you can see the stone-flagged laboratory where Faraday made many of his most important electrical discoveries.

The museum is in the basement of the Royal Institution in Mayfair where Faraday, the son of a blacksmith, became first a lab assistant and then professor of chemistry.

---

**Michael Faraday Museum**
*Open 13.00-16.00 Tue & Thur.* Admission charge.
Guided tours.
⟨&⟩ Full access
⊖ Green Park

---

## Museum of Artillery in the Rotunda

Repository Road, Woolwich SE18. 081-316 5402.

Begun in 1778 and stored at Woolwich, home of the Royal Artillery since 1805, the Museum of Artillery is the historic weapons collection of the Royal Artillery and the finest ordnance collection in Britain. Housed in and around an extraordinary, circular, tent-like structure originally built for the St James's Park peace celebrations of 1814 and given to the Regiment as a home for military curiosities in 1819, it contains all kinds of guns and weapons, mainly artillery, dating back to medieval times. Although most of the guns were used in battle or designed to be so used, there are also many small models and full-size experimental pieces which help show how artillery has developed over the centuries – both in Britain and abroad. The rarer and more precious pieces are displayed inside the Rotunda. Outside, in the grounds, you can see larger guns dating from the First World War and later. The Royal Artillery Regimental Museum (see page 76) is nearby.

---

**Museum of Artillery in the Rotunda**
*Open Apr-Oct 12.00-17.00 Mon-Fri, 13.00-17.00 Sat & Sun; Nov-Mar 12.00-16.00 Mon-Fri, 13.00-16.00 Sat & Sun.* Admission free. Shop. Guided tours. Guidebook. Research facilities.
*Refreshments*: Vending machines dispensing hot & cold drinks.
&#9855; Partial access
&#8734; Woolwich Arsenal (then bus 53)

---

## Museum of Garden History

St Mary-at-Lambeth, Lambeth Palace Road SE1.        4 G6
071-261 1891.

Cos lettuce, acacia, lilac and many other plants common in Britain today were brought to this country in the 17thC by John Tradescant and his son, also John, both gardeners to royalty and intrepid travellers. They propagated their discoveries in the garden of their home in Lambeth, while in their house was displayed their famous collection of curiosities, dubbed Tradescant's Ark. When they died (John senior in 1638 and John junior in 1662) they were buried in a joint tomb in the parish church, next door to Lambeth Palace, official London home of the Archbishop of Canterbury.

In the 1970s the church was deconsecrated and the Tradescant Trust was set up to turn it into a museum of garden history. When the museum is properly established it will have permanent displays on a new first-floor level to be inserted into the church. In the meantime, it has set out some temporary displays alongside the shop and lecture area giving a brief overview of the development of gardening in England. Also on show is a collection of antique gardening implements and the original wrought-iron gateway of Tradescant's Ark.

Outside in the old churchyard you can see the tomb of the Tradescants (and of Admiral Bligh of Mutiny on the *Bounty* fame) and a small replica 17thC garden growing plants of the period. The genus *tradescantia* is named after the Tradescants.

---

**Museum of Garden History**
*Open Mar-mid Dec 11.00-15.00 Mon-Fri, 10.30-17.00 Sun.*
Admission free.
Shop. Guided tours.
*Refreshments*: Café serving hot & cold snacks.
*Educational facilities*: Gardening courses, lectures.
&#9855; Partial access
&#9897; Waterloo (then bus 159, 77), Victoria (then bus 507)

---

## Museum of the Honourable Artillery Company

Armoury House, City Road EC1. 071-606 4644.                2 D3

Founded in 1537 by City merchants and traders, the Honourable Artillery Company is the oldest regiment in the British Army and the senior unit of the Territorial Army. Originally its members trained in the use of long-bows, cross-bows and hand-held firearms – collectively known as 'artillery'. Training with cannon started in 1670. The Company came to this site – with its 5 acres (2ha) of playing fields enclosed by buildings on the north side of the City – in 1641 and had its present headquarters built in 1735. Inside, one room on the ground floor has been set aside as a museum. Here, besides finding out more about the history of the regiment (it first saw active service overseas in the Boer War), you can see swords, muskets and other weapons; red, green, blue and buff uniforms of the 19thC and 20thC, accoutrements such as pouches and sabertaches; and an interesting head-dress collection, including two very fine Grenadiers' caps worn in the early 18thC.

---

**Museum of the Honourable Artillery Company**
*Open by appointment 09.30-17.30 Mon-Fri.* Admission free,
donations welcome.
&#9855; Full access. Toilet.
&#9897; Old Street

---

## Museum of London

London Wall EC2. 071-600 3699.                2 E6

Founded in 1976 by the amalgamation of two older museums, the Museum of London covers the social history and physical

*Roman kitchen, Museum of London*

development of the capital from prehistoric times to the Second World War. It is housed in a modern building at the north-west corner of what was the walled city, and overlooks an exposed section of the medieval wall which is treated, by means of a clever viewing gallery, as one of its exhibits. A courtyard garden in the centre of the museum – open in summer and visible through glass walls at other times of year – forms another outdoor exhibit, this time presenting in living form London's extensive nursery trade from medieval times to the 20thC.

Encircling the courtyard are two levels of display areas. Each one is split into chronological sections, and the first starts with a look at what and who were in the London area before London itself. Within each section there are features on subjects as diverse as architecture, the Court, death and burial, docks, education, firefighting, hospitals, immigration, industry, pageantry and public services.

The range of exhibits is amazing. As well as pictures, models, maps and reconstructions, there are things from every era in the city's history including a wonderful Bronze Age shield, and a mosaic floor and exquisite jewellery from Roman times. From the 17thC there are two complete period rooms and the fabulous Cheapside hoard, a Jacobean jeweller's stock-in-trade discovered under a cellar floor in 1912. The 18thC and later are represented by period clothes, dolls' houses, old prison cells and shop interiors, a huge, bright group portrait of a galaxy of Edwardian music-hall performers by Walter Lambert, and several vehicles, including the Lord Mayor's Coach. This fantastic 2-ton concoction of the 18thC, all gilt and crimson, is brought out once a year for the Lord Mayor's Show in November. In short, there is something here to interest everybody, and the museum should be a regular place of pilgrimage for every Londoner.

---

**Museum of London**
*Open 10.00-18.00 Tue-Sat & Bank Hols, 14.00-18.00 Sun.*
Admission charge (free *after 16.30*).
Shop. Guided tours. Guidebook. Films. Research facilities.
Organised walks around London.
*Refreshments*: Terrace Café licensed restaurant serving hot & cold meals and light snacks *10.00-17.00 Mon-Sat, 12.00-17.00 Sun.*
Lunch served *12.00-14.30 Mon-Sun.* Outdoor seating in *summer.*
*Educational facilities*: Tours for schools, worksheets, lectures, workshops.
&#9855; Full access. Toilet.
&#9400; Barbican, St Paul's

---

## Museum of Mankind

6 Burlington Gardens W1. 071-323 8043.                    4 D3
The 12-room Museum of Mankind in Mayfair houses the anthropological collections of the British Museum's Department of Ethnography. The finest of its kind in the world, there are hundreds of thousands of objects, old and new, illustrating many different aspects of the art and life of indigenous cultures all over the world. The emphasis is on the Americas, Africa, the Middle East, Australia, the Pacific Islands and parts of Asia. Apart from some Bulgarian costumes and shadow puppets from Turkey and Greece, there is almost nothing in the museum from Europe.

Some of the highlights of the collection are Navajo blankets, Cherokee baskets and Inuit sleds and hunting equipment from North America; Olmec jade carvings and Aztec and Maya sculptures from South America; Yoruba masks, Asante gold ornaments and Zulu beadwork from Africa; a Bedouin tent and Palestinian Arab costume from the Middle East; Tibetan textiles and great copper trumpets from Asia; and boomerangs, Maori cloaks, shark-tooth weapons, coconut-fibre armour and an Easter Island statue from Oceania.

Many of these objects, particularly the older ones, were collected by travellers, explorers and colonial administrators in the days of empire. A spectacular mourning dress from Tahiti, for example, was presented to Captain Cook on his second voyage. The Javanese puppets came from Sir Stamford Raffles of Singapore fame. Earlier in his life he had been Lieutenant-Governor of Java. Many modern objects, like the 1986 Aboriginal painting *Bush Potato Dreaming*, have been gathered by museum staff on rescue missions to save artefacts from cultures under threat or on the verge of extinction.

When you visit the museum, it's important to bear in mind that, with one exception, the room displays all change fairly frequently, even in the Introduction to the Collections room on the ground floor and in the Treasures Room on the first floor. The only permanent display (in Room 3 on the ground floor) features a small but wonderful collection of Aztec wooden objects, decorated with turquoise mosaics and made in our 15thC or early 16thC.

---

**Museum of Mankind**
*Open 10.00-17.00 Mon-Sat, 14.30-18.00 Sun.* Admission free.
Shop. Films. Research facilities.
*Refreshments*: Café de Colombia serving hot & cold light meals and snacks *10.30-16.30 Mon-Sat, 14.30-17.00 Sun.*
*Educational facilities*: Tours for schools, worksheets, lectures, workshops.
&#9855; Full access. Toilet.
&#9901; Piccadilly Circus

---

## Museum of Methodism
49 City Road EC1. 071-253 2262.                    2 D3
The Museum of Methodism is in the undercroft of Wesley's Chapel, the mother church of Methodists worldwide. The chapel was built in 1778, just north of the City, and stands next to Wesley's House (see page 138) where the founder of Methodism, John Wesley, lived for the last 12 years of his life.

In the museum, numbered panels with words and pictures and various pieces of Wesleyana tell the story of John Wesley and his brother Charles, outlining the development of their church, from its beginnings at Oxford in the 1720s up to the present day. Alongside the main historical exhibition, satellite displays look at different aspects of Methodism, such as the various branches of the church, what Methodists believe and how Methodists are distributed around the globe.

John Wesley's tomb is in the churchyard outside the chapel. Wesley's mother – along with many non-conformist heroes like John Bunyan and William Blake – lies in Bunhill Fields cemetery across the road.

---

**Museum of Methodism**
*Open 10.00-16.00 Mon-Sat.* Admission charge.
Shop. Guided tours. Guidebook. Films. Research facilities.
*Educational facilities*: Tours for schools, worksheets, lectures.
🔆 Partial access – ground floor only.
⊖ Old Street

---

## Museum of the Moving Image (MOMI)
South Bank SE1. 071-928 3535.                                    5 B4

Tucked neatly under Waterloo Bridge in a special modern building, MOMI is a highly successful museum telling the story of cinema and television. The museum is laid out chronologically so you start your tour with Oriental shadow play and other early attempts at making images move. Then, following the yellow-brick direction arrows, you move through the invention of photography and moving pictures, the early days of cinema, Hollywood and the growth of television, finishing up in a life-size TV studio displaying the latest in computer graphics. Sets like this, which help put in context the museum's diverse exhibits, ranging from magic lanterns to huge movie cameras, are one of the features of MOMI. Besides the TV studio, you will also pass through an early cinema foyer showing silent films and describing how the movie business developed around such names as Pathé and 20th Century Fox; a Russian cinema-train used for spreading communist propaganda; a Hollywood film studio with the workings of the different departments explained in little booths round the outside of the room; and the foyer of a 1930s Odeon chronicling the history of British cinema from the 1920s to Derek Jarman.

Apart from the well-designed sets, another strength of the museum is the way the designers, in contrast to the passive nature of screen viewing, have tried to involve visitors as much as possible. There are plenty of buttons to press and devices to play with, like the zoetrope and 'What the Butler Saw' machines in the early stages. And of course there are numerous screenings to watch, from newsreels of famous events like the Hindenburg airship disaster to a special Alf

Garnett show. In the Animation Room you can make your own cartoons, and in the TV studio practise reading the news to camera, or be interviewed by Barry Norman.

All the flashing lights, flickering screens and other electronic devices are managed from a control room in the centre of the museum. Itself one of the exhibits, you can see right inside, and ask the technicians how they keep track of everything in what is, technologically, the most sophisticated museum in the world. If you have questions elsewhere on your tour, put them to the well-informed actor-guides, who you will see patrolling the display areas dressed in character. But beware, they can be embarrassingly uninhibited!

---

**Museum of the Moving Image**
*Open 10.00-18.00 Mon-Sun.* Admission charge.
Shop *open to 19.30 Mon-Sun.* Guidebook. Films.
*Refreshments*: Licensed restaurant serving hot & cold light meals and snacks *12.00-17.30,* and full hot meals *17.30-21.00.* Coffee shop *open 10.00-21.00.* Bar *open 17.30-21.00.*
*Educational facilities*: Tours for schools, worksheets, lectures, workshops.
&#9855; Full access. Toilet.
&#1012; Embankment, Waterloo

---

### Museum of the Order of St John

St John's Gate, St John's Lane EC1. 071-253 6644.     2 D5
Hidden away in a little-known but historic part of London, the Museum of the Order of St John is one of London's most fascinating specialist museums. It is also an important and, for London, unusual historic building.

Essentially there are two small museums here. One deals with the medieval Order of St John, otherwise known as the Knights Hospitaller. The main displays illustrate the history of the international order, based successively in the Holy Land, Cyprus and Malta, and its English branch, based here in what was the priory of Clerkenwell. Smaller sections cover the historic St John's Gate building, the main entrance to Clerkenwell priory (demolished following the 16thC-suppression of the English order), and the local history of Clerkenwell. The other museum focuses on the St John Ambulance Brigade, the volunteer first aid organisation set up by the revived British Order of St John in the 19thC.

If you take the guided tour, you can also see the great hall and other principal rooms of the Gatehouse, now the headquarters of the modern Order, and the Grand Priory Church, the church of the modern Order. Beneath the church, the Norman crypt was part of the original medieval priory and is one of the few surviving Norman buildings in London.

---

**Museum of the Order of St John**
*Open 10.00-17.00 Mon-Fri, 10.00-16.00 Sat.* Admission free.
Guided tours of Grand Priory Church and Gatehouse *11.00 & 14.30 Tue, Fri & Sat.* Admission charge.
Shop. Guided tours. Guidebook. Research facilities.
&#9851; Partial access. Toilet.
&#9758; Farringdon

---

## Museum of the Royal Pharmaceutical Society of Great Britain

1 Lambeth High Street SE1. 071-735 9141.                    7 F2

Set up in 1842 and the only one of its kind in the country, the RPS museum covers all aspects of the history of pharmacy, with special emphasis on its evolution in Britain. It contains more than 45,000 objects in all, and a selection is on permanent display in the Society's modern building on the Surrey side of Lambeth Bridge. As well as old medicines and drugs dating from the 18thC, there are hundreds of colourful glass or china jars in china or glass for keeping leeches and storing potions; a fine collection of pharmaceutical delftware and other ceramics; pestles and mortars; weighing and measuring instruments; and masses of prints, paintings, photographs and general pharmaceutical ephemera. Because the collection is dotted around the RPS building visitors have to be guided personally, so unfortunately access has to be restricted to those with a serious interest in the subject.

---

**Museum of the Royal Pharmaceutical Society**
*Open by appointment only 09.00-17.00 Mon-Fri.* Admission free.
Guided tours. Research facilities.
&#9851; Full access. Toilet.
&#9758; Westminster, Lambeth North

---

## Museum of the United Grand Lodge of England

Freemasons' Hall, Great Queen Street WC2.                    4 F2
071-831 9811.

If you have ever wondered what freemasonry is and how it started, take a trip to Freemason's Hall, the headquarters of the premier lodge of both British and international freemasonry. Inside on the first floor, a bright and colourful exhibition outlines the history of the fraternity in England from its origins in the 16thC. A mass of masonic regalia and memorabilia is on show – dating mainly from the 18thC when the Craft was first formally organised – and includes many of those strange aprons masons wear, plus lots of badges, documents, paintings and engravings, silverware, glass and ceramics. The largest exhibits are three huge gilt and blue chairs made in 1791, the largest of the three being the throne of the Grand Master himself.

Passing through the rather gloomy library, you come to a large and equally gloomy museum room with a balcony all the way round. This contains the Lodge's main collections of plate, glass, porcelain and pottery, jewels and regalia, much of it of very high quality. To the layman the museum is not as appealing as the exhibition, but if you are interested in masonry or in fine craftsmanship, it has more than enough to keep you enthralled for hours.

---

**Museum of the United Grand Lodge of England**
*Open 10.00-17.00 Mon-Fri, 10.00-13.00 Sat. Closed Bank Hols and preceding Sat.* Admission free.
Shop. Guided tours of the Grand Temple inside Freemasons' Hall leave the museum *hourly between 11.00 and 16.00 Mon-Fri.* Guidebook. Research facilities.
&#9855; Full access
&#8854; Holborn

---

## Musical Museum

368 High Street, Brentford, Middlesex. 081-560 8108.

The Musical Museum in Brentford, just across the river from Kew Gardens, is a fine collection of automatic musical instruments, mainly self-playing pianos, dating from around the turn of the century. The beauty of this modest enterprise, started in 1963, is that you get to hear as well as see the historic instruments on show. During the 90-minute demonstration tour, which visitors are strongly encouraged to take to get the most out of the museum, the old church housing the collection resounds with the music of all manner of automatic organs, musical boxes and pianos. Some of the pianos, using special paper rolls and pneumatic systems, faithfully reproduce the playing of turn of the century composers and musicians like Rachmaninov and Sullivan. Reproducing pianos were succeeded by the phonograph and some early examples of these are on show as well. Also featured is a Wurlitzer theatre organ which, along with other instruments from the collection, is played in evening concerts held during the museum's summer opening season.

**Musical Museum**
*Open Jul & Aug 14.00-17.00 Wed-Sun; Apr-Jun & Sep-Oct 14.00-17.00 Sat & Sun. Closed Nov-Mar.* Admission charge.
Shop. Guided tours. Guidebook.
♿ No access
⊖ Gunnersbury (then bus 237, 267)

## National Army Museum
Royal Hospital Road SW3. 071-730 0717.                    6 F4
In a modern building next to Chelsea Hospital where many military veterans have lived out their last days, the National Army Museum tells the story of the British Army. The chronicle starts in 1485 when the Yeomen of the Guard were first raised, and carries on through the heady days of imperial expansion right up to the Falklands War and the present day. Indeed the museum is so current that relics of the Gulf War were on display within weeks of the ending of the conflict.

The museum's displays focus deliberately on what it was actually like to be a British or Commonwealth soldier in peacetime and in war. Using videos, models and reconstructions as well as the huge amount of priceless militaria in its possession, the museum brings that personal experience alive. For those visitors to the museum, who have little or no direct experience of army life, let alone war, this will probably be the most interesting part of the museum. But there is also plenty to attract military history buffs interested in hard details of battles, campaigns, uniforms, weapons and medals.

The story of the army is presented in a special gallery on the middle level of the museum. Next to it is the 'Road to Waterloo' Gallery featuring a 400sq ft model of the battle containing 70,000 tiny soldiers. On the upper level are the uniform gallery and the art gallery with its stirring battle scenes and military portraits by famous artists. The Duke of Marlborough by Kneller is here, and there are later portraits by Gainsborough, Reynolds, Lawrence and others. The most curious and somehow pathetic exhibit in the museum is the skeleton of Napoleon's horse, Marengo.

On the ground level along with the the shop and café are the special exhibitions areas and weapons gallery, the latter showing the small arms carried by soldiers during the last five centuries, from longbows to machine guns. Down in the basement there is a large collection of regimental silver, much of it from disbanded Irish regiments. As yet no large vehicles or artillery pieces are on display.

> **National Army Museum**
> *Open 10.00-17.30 Mon-Sun.* Admission free.
> Shop *open from 12.00 Mon-Sun.* Guided tours. Guidebook. Films. Research facilities.
> *Refreshments*: Café serving drinks & snacks.
> *Educational facilities*: Tours for schools, worksheets, films, workshops.
> &#9855; Full access. Toilet.
> &#9740; Sloane Square

## National Hearing Aid Museum

Royal National Throat, Nose and Ear Hospital,          5 B1
Grays Inn Road WC1. 071-837 8855 x 4220.
A small but representative collection of ear trumpets, speaking tubes, oracles and other hearing aids dating from the late 18thC to the present day. The devices are exhibited in showcases, each with an explanatory panel, along one side of a corridor on the third floor of the Audiology Centre at the Throat, Nose and Ear Hospital. On the other side hang illustrations showing how the various hearing aids were used, and some of the ingenious techniques adopted for concealing them.

> **National Hearing Aid Museum**
> *Open by appointment 09.00-17.00 Mon-Fri.* Admission free.
> &#9855; Full access. Toilet.
> &#9740; King's Cross

## National Maritime Museum and Queen's House

Romney Road, Greenwich SE10. 081-858 4422.
Being an island, Britain has always had a special relationship with the sea. For centuries the country has depended on it for food, trade, defence and links with other countries, including the overseas empire. Opened in 1937 in what was a school for the children of naval pensioners in Greenwich Hospital, the National Maritime Museum at Greenwich tells the story of that relationship. It starts with Henry VIII and the founding of the Royal Navy and continues up to the present day, looking at the commercial and leisure aspects of the subject as well as the military.

Building on old collections like the Admiralty's technical archive begun about 1720, the museum has assembled the finest maritime record in the world. Spanning 2000 years of sea and river travel, it contains everything from maps and

*National Maritime Museum from Greenwich Park*

charts, dramatic paintings and model boats, to royal barges and steam launches and the personal possessions of Nelson, Cook and other naval heroes. Unfortunately, the museum is not big enough to display real ships, but in the Neptune Gallery you can explore a complete steam-paddle tug, by far the largest exhibit on show.

All this rich maritime heritage is displayed on three levels. Starting at the top, the first two take the story from the age of discovery in the 16thC through to the Napoleonic Wars and Arctic exploration in the 19thC. The lower level portrays the development of the boat from prehistoric times to the age of shipbuilding in iron and steel. To guide you in your tour, we list below the various galleries and their contents, level by level, starting at the top.

| Level | Display | Highlights |
|-------|---------|-----------|
| **Upper** | **Discovery and Sea-Power 1450-1700** | Longbow and other artefacts from the 16thC *Mary Rose*. |
| | **Sea-Power** | Battle of Jutland and World War II (under construction). |
| | **The Ship of War 1650-1815** | Unrivalled collection of about 30 18thC Navy Board models, ranging in size from small longboats to 100-gun warships. |
| | **Captain Cook – Explorer** | |
| **Middle** | **Exploring the Arctic** | Tinned food and other relics of Sir John Franklin's ill-fated north-west passage expedition of 1847. |
| | **Surveying an Empire** | |
| | **18thC Trade and Communications** | Contemporary model of 1738 East Indiaman. |
| | **French Revolutionary Wars 1793-1815** | De Louthenbourg's famous painting of *The Battle of the 1st June 1794*. |
| | **Nelson Gallery** | Nelson's bullet-holed and blood-stained uniform. Turner's great painting of *The Battle of Trafalgar*. |
| **Lower** | **Neptune Hall** | The tug *Reliant* (1907). Boatshed and sail-loft sets. |
| | **Royal Barge House** | Prince Frederick's Barge, 1732. |
| | **Wooden Shipbuilding and Archaeology** | Reconstructions of three early boat discoveries in Britain. |
| | **Yachting** | |
| | **The Way of a Ship** | Six excellent audio-visual displays on crafts and lore of the sea. The fully-rigged HMS *Cornwallis*, the largest period model in the museum. |

Next to the museum, and attached to it by a colonnade, is the 17thC **Queen's House**, a royal palace designed by Inigo Jones and the first classical house to be built in England. Probably its most unusual feature is that it was built right over the Deptford to Woolwich road, hence the ground level passage continues on from the colonnade through the middle of the house.

There is an exhibition on the history of the house in the brick vaults of the basement, together with the Maritime Museum's treasury of gold and silver plate and other valuable objects. The ground floor, the heart of which is the Great Hall, a magnificent 40ft (12m), is used as a picture gallery for the Maritime Museum's huge collection of marine paintings – some English but most Netherlandish – showing the complete development of the genre from the 16thC to the 18thC. The father and son team of Van de Veldes, who had a studio in the house in 1675, are well represented.

Climbing the Tulip stairs, so-called because of the tulip motif in the wrought-iron balustrade, you come to the first-floor royal apartments. These are divided into two matching suites of rooms containing presence chamber, privy chamber, bedchamber and assorted anterooms and closets. One was for the king, the other for the queen. Both decorated and furnished as they were in 1662 when Queen Henrietta Maria lived in the palace.

The king's apartments were rarely used and so were simply furnished. This is how you see them today (with the notable exception of the blue and gold Presence Chamber). The queen's apartments were a proper home and therefore far more luxurious. All the rooms have different colour schemes – crimson and gold, shades of green, purple and silver, white and gold – and most are hung with specially woven reproduction silk damask wall hangings. The 17thC paintings show people connected with the house during the time of the Stuarts.

---

**National Maritime Museum**
*Open Apr-Sep 10.00-18.00 Mon-Sat, 14.00-18.00 Sun; Oct-Mar 10.00-17.00 Mon-Sat, 14.00-17.00 Sun.* Admission charge (a Passport ticket provides admission to the National Maritime Museum, the Queen's House, the Old Royal Observatory and the *Cutty Sark*, all in Greenwich).
Shop. Guided tours. Guidebook. Research facilities.
*Refreshments*: Café with hot & cold buffet *open Apr-Sep 10.00-17.00 Mon-Sat, 13.30-17.00 Sun; Oct-Mar 10.00-16.30 Mon-Sat, 13.30-16.30 Sun.*
*Educational facilities*: Tours for schools, worksheets, lectures, workshops.
&#9855; Partial access. Toilet. Information sheet available.
&#8612; Greenwich

**Queen's House**
*Open Apr-Sep 10.00-18.00 Mon-Sat, 12.00-18.00 Sun; Oct-Mar
10.00-17.00 Mon-Sat, 14.00-17.00 Sun.* Admission charge (see
details of Passport ticket above).
Shop. Guided tours. Guidebook. Research facilities.
*Refreshments*: Café with hot & cold buffet *open Apr-Sep 10.00-
17.00 Mon-Sat, 13.30-17.00 Sun; Oct-Mar 10.00-16.30 Mon-Sat,
13.30-16.30 Sun.*
*Educational facilities*: Tours for schools, worksheets, lectures,
workshops.
🦽 Partial access – Royal apartments inaccessible. Information
   sheet available. Toilet.
⭢ Greenwich

## National Postal Museum
King Edward Building, King Edward Street EC1.                5 D2
071-239 5420.
The National Postal Museum was founded in 1965 and
contains one of the world's greatest philatelic collections.
Apart from some pretty stamp boxes and other postal relics,
not to mention old letter boxes kept in store, it consists mostly
of stamps and is housed in a large room above London's chief
post office near St Paul's. In the pull-out cases on the left-
hand-side you can see all the designs for British stamps,
including designs for stamps which were never issued, like
Edward VIII's coronation set. Here, also, you can see a
complete collection of all stamps issued throughout the world
since 1878 (when the Universal Postal Union was established).
There are also many foreign stamps issued before that date.
    The pull-out cases down the middle contain the mainstay
of the museum's holdings, the Reginald Phillips collection
of Victorian stamps. Among the many developments this
collection documents, the most important is the story of the
Penny Black. In the pull-out cases and in the display cases
down the right-hand side of the room you can see whole
sheets of Penny Blacks, not to mention Penny Reds and
Twopenny Blues too. All come from the Phillips collection
and they are an amazing sight for anyone who remembers
hungering for just one specimen of these rarities in their
juvenile stamp-collecting days.

**National Postal Museum**
*Open 09.30-16.30 Mon-Thur, to 16.00 Fri.* Admission free.
Shop. Guided tours. Guidebook. Films. Research facilities.
*Educational facilities*: Tours for schools, worksheets, lectures.
🦽 No access, unless advance notice of visit provided.
⊖ St Paul's

**Natural History Museum**
Cromwell Road SW7. 071-938 9123.  6 D1
One of Britain's great national collections, the Natural
History Museum covers the story of the earth and all living
creatures, including extinct life forms, and human beings.
Originally a section of the British Museum and housed in
Bloomsbury, the collection expanded dramatically through
19thC research and exploration and moved to this newly constructed building by Alfred Waterhouse, in South Kensington,
in 1881. The impressive façade, in pale terracotta and slate
blue, is ornamented with animal figures; those on the western
wing depict living forms, while those on the eastern wing are

*Natural History Museum*

# Natural History Museum

**Second Floor**

British natural history

Mineral deposits of the world
Mineral deposits of the world
Building stones

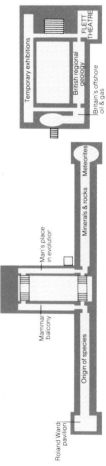

**First Floor**

Roland Ward pavilion

Origin of species

Mammal balcony

Man's place in evolution

Minerals & rocks

Meteorites

Temporary exhibitions

British regional geology

Britain's offshore oil & gas

FLETT THEATRE

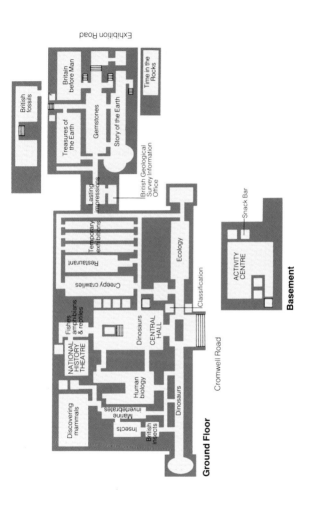

Exhibition Road

British fossils

Britain before Man

Time in the Rocks

Treasures of the Earth

Gemstones

Story of the Earth

Lasting impressions

British Geological Survey Information Office

Temporary exhibitions

Restaurant

Creepy crawlies

Ecology

Classification

Fishes amphibians & reptiles

Dinosaurs

NATIONAL HISTORY THEATRE

CENTRAL HALL

Discovering mammals

Human biology

Marine invertebrates

Insects

British insects

Dinosaurs

Cromwell Road

**Ground Floor**

Snack Bar

ACTIVITY CENTRE

**Basement**

extinct. Many of the exhibits, and the way they are shown, date from the time of the museum's foundation, but for two decades now the museum has been modernising itself, building fun and state-of-the-art permanent exhibitions, so that what we have today is not only the largest natural history collection in the world, but also one of the most up-to-date and exciting.

Using hands-on exhibits and advanced technology like computers and videos, the museum goes far beyond its Victorian predecessor in its mission to demonstrate not only the essential diversity of the natural world, but also to explain some of the scientific principles underlying it, such as how natural forms have evolved, and how living things interact with each other and with their non-living surroundings.

The museum is divided into two sections, the Life Galleries and the Earth Galleries. This division reflects the fact that until a few years ago the Earth Galleries were a separate Geological Museum in an adjacent building. The Geological Museum was founded as an offshoot of the Geological Survey in 1835.

The main entrance in Cromwell Road leads into the cathedral-like central hall of the Life Galleries. Dominating the space here is the plaster-cast skeleton of the dinosaur Diplodocus, one of the largest animals ever to walk the earth and the centrepiece of a permanent dinosaur exhibition (the original is in the Carnegie Museum in Pittsburgh). There are several other permanent exhibitions in the Life Galleries, plus interesting changing displays.

Access to the Earth Galleries is either from the ground floor of the Life Galleries or by the old main entrance to the Geological Museum round the corner in Exhibition Road. Like the Life Galleries, the Earth Galleries are arranged over all three floors, and contain both permanent exhibitions and other displays.

As you walk around the Life Galleries, spend a little time looking at the building as well as the specimens. Alfred Waterhouse's Romanesque temple of science and nature, with wild flower decoration all over the walls and high curved   ceiling is, in its way, every bit as remarkable as the museum.

**PERMANENT EXHIBITIONS AND HIGHLIGHTS**

***Ground floor***

*Ecology*
A dramatic voyage of discovery through our living planet – plenty of audience participation.

*Dinosaurs*
Skeletons and models of dinosaurs, including Diplodocus.

*Human Biology*
Discover more about your body and how it works.

*Discovering Mammals*
Living and fossil mammals, from land and sea, including a life-sized model of the great blue whale.

*Creepy Crawlies*
Hundreds of insects, spiders and centipedes – arthropods to the initiated.

*Treasure of the Earth*
The earth's minerals, how man obtains and uses them.

*Story of the Earth*
Experience the tremors of an earthquake in the simulator and see the moon rock.

*Gemstones*
3000 cut and polished stones, with crystals and rough specimens as well.

**First floor**

*Origin of species*
A fascinating exposition of Darwin's theory of natural selection.

*Man's place in evolution*
How we are related to fossil men and women.

*Britain's offshore oil and gas*
Designed like an offshore oil rig on two decks – there's also a film about the geological history of oil and gas.

---

**Natural History Museum**
*Open 10.00-18.00 Mon-Sat, 11.00-18.00 Sun.* Admission charge (free *16.30-18.00 Mon-Fri, 17.00-18.00 Sat, Sun & Bank Hols*, and for children under 5).
Shop. Guided tours. Guidebook. Films. Research facilities.
*Refreshments*: Museum Restaurant, licensed, serving hot & cold meals from a changing menu. Waterhouse Café serving coffee, tea, sandwiches and pastries *11.00-17.00 Mon-Sat, 14.30-17.00 Sun.* Tuck shop; snacks for school parties *11.00-15.30.*
*Educational facilities*: Tours for schools, worksheets, lectures, workshops, activity centre.
&#9855; Full access. Toilets.
&#9678; South Kensington

## Normanby College Library

King's College Hospital, Denmark Hill, Camberwell SE5.
071-326 3363.
Normanby College in Camberwell is a training college for
nurses, midwives, physiotherapists and similar medical
specialists. On the walls of the corridor outside the college
library there is a small exhibition chronicling, mainly in
words and pictures, the history of nursing in Camberwell from
the 1820s onwards. The first nursing school in the country,
pre-dating Florence Nightingale's better-known establishment
at St Thomas's by three years, was opened in the area by
Sister Mary Jones in 1857.

---
**Normanby College Library**
*Open 09.30-17.30 Mon-Fri.* Admission free.
&#9855; Full access
&#8733; Denmark Hill
---

## North Woolwich Old Station Museum

Pier Road, North Woolwich E16. 071-474 7244.
This mid-Victorian station in east London has been turned
into a museum illustrating the development of railways in the
eastern counties. Words, pictures, models, documents and
posters in the old waiting rooms and vestibule tell the story of
the various railway companies in the area, from the 19thC
Eastern Counties Railway to modern-day British Rail. Outside
you can see three steam engines, and a 1929 Gresley coach,
built at the local coachworks in Stratford. The oldest locomotive, kept in the old turntable pit, is an 1876 shunting engine.
The other two are post-World War II industrial engines. Both
worked on local lines and one of them can be seen puffing
away on the line next to the station platform on the first
Sunday in every month from March to October.

---
**North Woolwich Old Station Museum**
*Open 10.00-17.00 Mon-Wed & Sat, 14.00-17.00 Sun & Bank Hols.*
Admission free.
Shop. Guided tours.
*Educational facilities*: Tours for schools, worksheets.
&#9855; Full access
&#8733; Woolwich
---

## Old Royal Observatory

Greenwich Park, Greenwich SE10. 081-858 4422.
Up on the hill behind the Queen's House and the National
Maritime Museum in Greenwich stands the Old Royal
Observatory, a museum of astronomy and time – two

concepts closely linked to navigation. Indeed, the Observatory was set up by Charles II in 1675 with the express object of finding an astronomical method for sailors to establish longitude. The breakthrough eventually came a century later, but through developments in accurate timekeeping rather than astronomy. The world's first really accurate timekeepers were invented in the 18thC by John Harrison, a carpenter's son from Lincolnshire. Examples of his famous chronometers are on show in Flamsteed House, one of the two buildings which make up the Observatory.

Designed by Sir Christopher Wren, Flamsteed House was used by the first Astronomer Royal, the Reverend John Flamsteed, and his successors until the Observatory moved to Herstmonceux, Sussex in 1948. The main room in the house was the first-floor Octagon Room. Its shape and height allowed the early astronomers to view the heavens through their long telescopes. Directly below you can see the 17thC apartments of the Astronomer Royal – four small panelled rooms, plainly decorated and furnished in the style of the period. Adjacent galleries tell the story of the measurement of time (including Greenwich Mean Time – GMT) with one of the finest collections of scientific instruments in the country. In 1833 a scarlet time ball was erected on a mast on top of the house as a guide to shipping on the Thames; it is still dropped at precisely 1pm each day.

In the Meridian Building next to Flamsteed House the displays, including a large collection of telescopes, focus on the development of astronomy from the 17thC onwards. In the centre is Airy's Transit Circle, the mid-19thC telescope that defines the Greenwich meridian. Then, in the dome right at the top of the building, you can see the huge refracting telescope – the largest of its kind in Britain and the seventh largest in the world – which was used at Herstmonceux until only 20 years ago.

---

**Old Royal Observatory**
*Open Apr-Sep 10.00-18.00 Mon-Sat, 12.00-18.00 Sun; Oct-Mar 10.00-17.00 Mon-Sat, 14.00-17.00 Sun.* Admission charge (a Passport ticket provides admission to the National Maritime Museum, the Queen's House, the Old Royal Observatory and the *Cutty Sark*, all in Greenwich).
Shop. Guided tours. Guidebook. Research facilities.
*Refreshments*: Tea pavilion in Royal Park, with snacks and high teas.
*Educational facilities*: Tours for schools, worksheets, lectures, planetarium shows.
&#9855; Partial access. Information sheet available. Toilet adjacent to premises.
&#10137; Greenwich

## Old St Thomas's Hospital Operating Theatre and Herb Garret

9a St Thomas's Street SE1. 071-955 4791.                    5 E4

A medical museum with a difference, this is the old operating theatre of St Thomas's Hospital and the only operating theatre to survive from the days before anaesthetics and antiseptics. Complete with wooden operating table and tiered seats for medical students, it was in use from 1821 until 1862 when St Thomas's moved to Lambeth. The theatre was built in part of the hospital chapel loft where the hospital's apothecaries had traditionally stored their medicinal herbs. The part of the loft not used by the theatre (ie the remaining part of the old herb garret) now houses a display of surgical instruments, specimens and other gruesome medical relics.

---

**Old St Thomas's Hospital Operating Theatre and Herb Garret**
*Open 12.30-16.00 Mon, Wed & Fri.* Admission charge.
Guided tours. Guidebook. Research facilities.
*Educational facilities:* Tours for schools, worksheets, lectures.
&#x267F; No access
&#x2296; Waterloo

---

## Percival David Foundation of Chinese Art

53 Gordon Square WC1. 071-387 3909.                    1 F5

Anyone interested in Chinese art and ceramics should certainly visit this great collection, which is generally regarded as the finest outside China. The three galleries contain about 1700 pieces made during the Song, Yuan, Ming and Qing dynasties (10thC-18thC). As well as bowls, plates, teapots and cups, there are many other examples of the ceramicist's art: table screens, ink palettes and brush rests, incense burners and perfume baskets, garden seats and writing boxes, even a china flute and a hard-looking headrest. Amongst the most beautiful pieces are the tiny, exquisitely detailed figures of laughing buddhas and plump-cheeked, open-gowned scholars. Two large vases made in 1351 are the earliest blue and white pieces so far recorded, anywhere in the world.

The greater part of the collection was put together by the scholar Sir Percival David and presented, along with his library, to the University of London in 1950. In 1952, the year the Foundation opened to promote the study and teaching of Chinese art and culture, the Elphinstone gift added much fine monochrome porcelain of the 18thC. Many of the David pieces bear inscriptions which were applied either at the time of manufacture or later when in the possession of the emperor Qianlong. These are of immense historical value.

> **Percival David Foundation of Chinese Art**
> *Open 10.30-17.00 Mon-Fri.* Admission free.
> Guided tours. Guidebook. Research facilities.
> & Full access
> ⊖ Euston Square

## Peter Pan Gallery

Hospital for Sick Children, 55-57 Great Ormond          2 B5
Street WC1. 071-405 9200.
Part of the famous Great Ormond Street children's hospital,
the Peter Pan Gallery contains a small exhibition, in words
and pictures, on the history of the hospital, founded in 1852.
There are also a few artefacts, and several letters and articles
by the hospital's founder, Dr Charles West, and by two
famous authors, Charles Dickens and James Barrie. Dickens
publicised the work of the hospital and helped to raise money
when it got into financial difficulties. Barrie left it a regular
income in the form of the perpetual copyright of *Peter Pan*,
from which the gallery takes its name.

> **Peter Pan Gallery**
> *Open by appointment only 10.00-17.00 Mon-Fri.* Admission free.
> Research facilities.
> & No access
> ⊖ Holborn, Russell Square

## Polish Institute and Sikorski Museum

20 Princes Gate SW7. 071-589 9249.          3 F5
The Sikorski Museum is named after General Sikorski, the
wartime Polish prime minister and commander-in-chief who was
tragically killed in an aircrash in 1943. It contains personal effects
and papers relating to the General himself, and a large collection
of Polish militaria with exhibits going back several hundred years.
There are colours and banners, pre-war regimental badges and
uniforms, weapons, china, cutlery, photographs, trophies and
medals from regimental messes, 17thC cavalry armour and a
Turkish commanders' tent captured in 1621. The museum also
contains some paintings and engravings (not all military), bronze
sculptures, miniatures and 18thC Polish porcelain.

> **Polish Institute and Sikorski Museum**
> *Open 14.00-16.00 Mon-Fri, 10.00-16.00 first Sat of each month.*
> Admission free.
> Guided tours. Guidebook. Films. Research facilities.
> *Educational facilities:* Tours for schools, lectures.
> & No access
> ⊖ Knightsbridge (then bus 9, 10, 52, 52a), South Kensington (then
>   bus 49 or C1)

## Pollock's Toy Museum

1 Scala Street W1. 071-636 3452. 4 D1

Before his death in 1937, Benjamin Pollock was a maker of toy theatres and the last surviving publisher of the printed scenes and sets used in the theatres. The museum was started nearly 20 years after his death as a draw for the shop in Covent Garden where Pollock's toy theatres continued to be sold. Shop and museum moved to these two small 18thC houses off Tottenham Court Road in 1969.

You enter via 41 Whitfield Street, the ground floor of which is now the toy theatre shop. The toy museum is upstairs in a labyrinth of tiny rooms connected by narrow winding staircases. Each room has a different theme: puppets; optical, mechanical and constructional toys; dolls and dolls' houses; teddy bears; board games; tin toys and toy theatres. Small children find the atmosphere magical, and many of the exhibits, like an Egyptian clay mouse with moving parts made about 4000 years ago, are positioned at their level.

---

**Pollock's Toy Museum**
*Open 10.00-17.00 Mon-Sat.* Admission charge.
Shop (below museum, sells toy theatres). Guidebook. Research facilities.
*Educational facilities*: Tours for schools, lectures.
&#9855; No access
&#9681; Goodge Street

---

## Prince Henry's Room

17 Fleet Street EC4. 071-353 7323. 5 B2

This first-floor panelled room above an archway leading into the Inner Temple is remarkable because it is part of one of the few buildings to have escaped the Great Fire of 1666. The centrepiece of its fine plaster ceiling is an heraldic device of three feathers incorporating the initials PH. Both are thought to belong to James I's son Henry, who was created Prince of Wales in the same year the room was built – 1610. For this reason it has come to be called Prince Henry's Room. In those days it was the principal room of an inn called the Prince's Arms. Today, maintained by the City of London Corporation, it contains a small exhibition on the life of the famous diarist and naval administrator, Samuel Pepys (1633-1703), organised by the Samuel Pepys Society.

---

**Prince Henry's Room**
*Open 13.45-17.00 Mon-Fri.* Admission free.
Shop. Lectures.
&#9855; Partial access
&#9681; Blackfriars, St Paul's

---

**Public Record Office Museum**
Chancery Lane WC2. 081-876 3444.                    5 B2
A one-room exhibition of documents drawn from the 90 miles
of government archives. Aimed mainly at people interested in
family, local and community history, it is designed to bring
out the human dimension in official papers and focuses on
just a few examples in detail: the manor of Methwold in
Norfolk, Chertsey Abbey, the town of Sheffield, crown
servants, the Metropolitan Police, RAF aircrew and
operations, coalmining and miners, employment and health,
and the census. The most important historical document on
show is the *Domesday Book*, the great register of landowners
compiled under the orders of William the Conqueror in 1086.

---

**Public Record Office Museum**
*Open 10.00-17.00 Mon-Fri.* Admission free.
Shop. Guided tours. Guidebook. Research facilities.
*Educational facilities:* Tours for schools.
&#9855; Partial. Help provided if advance notice of visit given. Toilet.
&#9758; Chancery Lane, Temple

---

**Riesco Collection of Chinese Ceramics**
Fairfield Halls, Park Lane, Croydon, Surrey. 081-681 0821.
A nationally important collection put together by insurance
broker Raymond Riesco and bequeathed to the borough of
Croydon in 1959. It contains about 200 pieces, ranging in date
from the 3rdC BC to the late 18thC. As well as wares made
for household and burial use in China, there are ornamental
pieces made for export to the West and a number of pieces
made for the Chinese Imperial Court.

The collection is currently displayed in cases in the first-
floor Sun Lounge in Fairfield Halls arts and entertainment
centre. In 1994 it is due to move to a new Croydon Museum.

---

**Riesco Collection of Chinese Ceramics**
*Open 10.00-22.00 Mon-Sat and some Sun.* Admission free.
Shop.
*Refreshments:* Café serving light meals & snacks *10.30-20.30 Mon-Sat.*
&#9855; Full access. Toilet.
&#9837; East Croydon

---

**Rock Circus**
London Pavilion, Piccadilly Circus W1. 071-734 8025.     4 E3
Madame Tussaud's Rock Circus tells the story of rock and
pop from the days of Little Richard and Chuck Berry to

Michael Jackson and Jason Donovan. Donning headphones, you move through a series of tableaux featuring, in waxen form, the main stars of the last 30 years, some wearing clothes donated by their real life originals. Over the headphones come the songs that made them famous, linked together by a disc jockey's commentary. The coverage is fairly superficial, but a few interesting points come out. Did you know, for example, that Rod Stewart was a serious singer-songwriter before he became a larger-than-life rock star?

The main set of the first part of the show is a large studio room with disco lighting, a video wall and a central platform on which Elton John, Stevie Wonder and Little Richard slowly revolve. At one point Elvis rises out of the middle like Banquo's ghost only to disappear again in a cloud of stage smoke.

The highlight of the circus comes right at the end. Passing Robert Plant and ascending the Stairway to Heaven, you take your seat in a revolving auditorium. On stage, a greying Tim Rice hosts a rock show opened and closed by the Beatles as Sergeant Pepper's Lonely Hearts Club Band. The difference between this and the previous parts of the circus is that the 'bionic' models now move. Elvis curls his lip. Madonna shakes a tambourine. A stoned Janis Joplin struggles to her feet from a garden bench and wails out *Me and Bobby McGhee*. David Bowie drifts in space while singing an eerie *Major Tom*. The models, which move like string-less puppets, are a bit of a let down, but the music is great.

---

**Rock Circus**
*Open 11.00-21.00 Mon-Sun.* Admission charge.
Shop. Guidebook.
*Refreshments:* Vending machines selling drinks & confectionery.
*Educational facilities:* Tours for schools, worksheets.
&#9855; Full access, but only three wheelchairs allowed on the premises at any one time. Toilet.
&#9901; Piccadilly Circus

---

## Royal Air Force Museum
Grahame Park Way, Hendon NW9. 081-205 2266.
Britain's national museum of aviation stands on historic Hendon aerodrome in north-west London. Opened at the turn of the century, it was used for military aviation during World War I. Two large hangars dating from that time, and now linked together, form the main Aircraft Hall of the modern museum. Here you can see about 40 aircraft (slightly more

than half the total on show) spanning nearly 80 years of flying, including an early Blériot of the type that crossed the channel, and a prototype of the Lightning, a jet fighter retired from the RAF as recently as 1988. Also in the Aircraft Hall is a 14-seat flight simulator offering several different flight experiences. In one you are in a Tornado speeding through the Welsh mountains. In another, the Red Baron has you in his sights in a World War I dogfight.

Adjoining the main hall, 11 galleries tell the story of the RAF from the early days of flying right up to the present. Some of the galleries take the form of sets such as workshops, hangars, huts and lecture rooms complete with human dummies in uniform which allow the museum's exhibits – personal items as well as technical – to be displayed as realistically as possible. Galleries 1-3 and 7-11 are chronological. Among the contents of the other galleries are displays on Lord Trenchard and paintings by World War II artists.

Beyond the main hall two more large displays – museums in their own right – highlight the RAF's crucial role in defending Britain in World War II. *The Battle of Britain Experience* shows mainly the fighters and small fighter bombers – both German and British – of that time, plus a flying bomb and a V2 rocket. *Bomber Command* contains the big bombers like the Lancaster and the American Flying Fortress. It also takes a wider look at the overall development of aerial bombing, and among the 15 aircraft exhibited, includes a tiny World War I machine side by side with a giant modern Vulcan. One of the most poignant exhibits here is the

*Hawker Sea Fury, Royal Air Force Museum*

wreck of a Halifax shot down in an attack on the *Tirpitz* in 1942 and retrieved from the depths of a Norwegian lake 30 years later. Echoing the whole spirit of the museum – which is as much memorial as museum – it has been left unrestored as a silent tribute to the Bomber Command crews of World War II.

---

**Royal Airforce Museum**
*Open 10.00-18.00 Mon-Sun.* Admission charge.
Shop. Guided tours. Guidebook. Films. Research facilities.
*Refreshments:* Café, serving hot & cold snacks and meals *09.30-18.00 Mon-Sun.*
*Educational facilities:* Tours for schools, worksheets, lectures, workshops.
&#9855; Full access. Toilet.
&#10134; Colindale

---

## Royal Artillery Regimental Museum
Old Royal Military Academy, Woolwich SE18. 081-854 2242 x 5628.

The Royal Artillery has served in every one of the British Army's campaigns and theatres of operations since it was formed in 1716, so the regimental museum, housed in the central block of the Old Royal Military Academy in Woolwich, has a lot of ground to cover in chronicling the history of the regiment and its long military service over the past three centuries. 18thC campaigns, the Napoleonic Wars, the Crimean War, the Indian Mutiny, colonial and Boer Wars, the First and Second World Wars; Royal Horse, Mountain and Volunteer Artillery, land-based anti-aircraft artillery – they all feature in the excellent, chronologically-arranged displays in the three main rooms that make up the museum space. For guidance on the museum's overall layout, as well as a brief history of the Gunners, watch the introductory video at the entrance before beginning your tour. The Royal Artillery's weapons collection is housed in the nearby Museum of Artillery in the Rotunda (see page 47).

---

**Royal Artillery Regimental Museum**
*Open 12.30-16.30 Mon-Fri, 14.00-16.00 Sat & Sun. Closed Christmas Eve-New Year. Sometimes closes unexpectedly, so phone to check times in advance.* Admission free.
Shop. Sound guide. Guidebook.
&#9855; No access
&#8916; Woolwich Arsenal

---

**Royal College of Music Museum of Instruments**

Prince Consort Road SW7. 071-589 3643. 3 E6

Built up since the foundation of the College in 1883, the historic instrument collection at the Royal College of Music is one of the most important in the world. Housed in a special museum room opened in 1970 it contains nearly 500 individual pieces. Most are keyboard, wind and stringed instruments made in Europe over the past 500 years, but about 100 come from China, Japan, India, the Middle East and Africa. One of the African instruments is a blood-stained war horn from the Kings of the Ashantis. Musically and historically, the most interesting items are a German clavicytherium of about 1480 (the earliest surviving stringed keyboard instrument), an early harpsichord made in Venice in 1531, Handel's spinet, Haydn's clavichord, and trombones used by Elgar and Holst.

---

**Royal College of Music Museum of Instruments**
*Open termtime 14.00-16.30 Wed. Other times by appointment only.*
Admission charge.
Guided tours. Guidebook. Research facilities.
*Educational facilities*: Tours for schools.
🚻 Partial access
➎ Knightsbridge (then bus 9, 10, 52, 52a), South Kensington (then bus 49 or C1)

---

**Royal Hospital Chelsea**

Royal Hospital Road SW3. 071-730 0161. 6 G3

The Royal Hospital Chelsea was established by Charles II as a home for old soldiers, and was completed to the designs of Sir Christopher Wren in 1692. It is still in use today, the resident Pensioners easily recognisable by their old-fashioned uniforms, blue in winter, red in summer. The Hospital museum is housed in the single-storey Secretary's office next to the main building.

The Entrance Hall is dedicated to the memory of the great Duke of Wellington (1769-1852), and besides portraits of the duke, contains the table on which his body lay in state, and prints and paintings of the Battle of Waterloo (1815), including a vast canvas by George Jones. In the Long Gallery every exhibit illustrates some facet of the Hospital's life and history. On the walls are old maps, plans, photographs and engravings of the Hospital and pictures and prints of Pensioners uniforms. In the cases, or elsewhere in the room you can see real uniforms, muskets and swords, historic documents, bombs and war trophies, and old relics of

Hospital life like the great leathern beer jugs known as jacks. The Medal Room at one end of the Gallery has a very large collection of medals and cap badges once worn by Pensioners.

Besides the museum, you can also see the Hospital grounds and its panelled Great Hall and Chapel. The panelling in the hall is covered with the names of the world-wide campaigns fought by the British Army during the past 300 years.

---

**Royal Hospital Chelsea**
*Open Apr-Sep 10.00-12.00 & 14.00-16.00 Mon-Sat, 14.00-16.00 Sun; Oct-Mar 10.00-12.00 & 14.00-16.00 Mon-Sat.* Admission free.
Shop. Guided tours.
🚻 Partial access
🚇 Sloane Square

---

## Royal London Hospital Archives Centre and Museum

St Augustine with St Philip's Church, Newark Street, Whitechapel E1. 071-377 7000 x 3364.

The London Hospital was founded in 1740 and was the first hospital in England to have its own medical college. For two-and-a-half centuries it has been a landmark in the East End. The Archives Centre, in the crypt of a converted church at the back of the hospital, has an excellent exhibition about its history and work. Special sections cover different departments and some of the well-known people connected with the hospital, such as Edith Cavell – the nurse shot by the Germans for helping captured Resistance fighters in the First World War, and Dr John Barnardo. Both trained at the London.

In the display cases you can see some of Nurse Cavell's personal possessions, including her watercolour sketch book; various hospital artefacts such as early anaesthetic masks, a pewter bleeding bowl and a grisly 18thC amputation saw and knife. Among the hospital records is a patients' register of 1886 recording the admission of Joseph Merrick, better known as the Elephant Man. It was here that he spent the last four years of his tragic life under the care of Sir Frederick Treves.

---

**Royal London Hospital Archives Centre and Museum**
*Open by appointment 10.00-16.30 Mon-Fri.* Admission free, donation appreciated.
Shop. Guided tours. Guidebook. Research facilities.
*Educational facilities*: Tours for schools, worksheets, lectures.
🚻 Full access
🚇 Whitechapel

## Royal Mews

Buckingham Palace Road SW1. 071-799 2331.          4 C6

Built in 1823-4, the Royal Mews is a working stableyard attached to Buckingham Palace. Here the Queen stables her carriage horses and garages all her chief ceremonial coaches. Seven in number, they include the magnificent Gold State Coach made for George III in 1762. This 4-ton gilded and painted monster, which needs eight horses to pull it, has been used for every coronation since that of George IV in 1821. Also on show here are superb examples of Georgian and Victorian horse harness from the State Harness collection, probably the finest of its kind in the world; historic and ornate presentation saddles; and a fascinating display of photographs showing members of the royal family at work and play.

---

**Royal Mews**
*Open Apr-mid Jul 12.00-16.00 Wed & Thur; mid Jul-Sep 12.00-16.00 Wed-Fri; Oct-Mar 12.00-16.00 Wed only.* Admission charge.
Shop. Guidebook.
*Educational facilities*: Tours for schools.
&#x267F; Full access. Toilet.
&#x2296; Green Park, Hyde Park, Victoria

---

## Royal Military School of Music

Kneller Hall, Kneller Road, Twickenham, Middlesex. 081-898 5533.

A two-room museum housing the historic instrument collection of the Royal Military School of Music, where army bandsmen and bandmasters are trained. It contains about 80 woodwind and 60 brass instruments, plus a few stringed instruments, dating from the 18thC to the present day. Also to be seen are an organ that once belonged to Queen Victoria, and some portraits by Sir Godfrey Kneller, in whose one-time country home the Military School of Music has been based since its foundation in 1857. The house was built in 1709 and then completely refashioned as a neo-Jacobean mansion in 1848.

---

**Royal Military School of Music**
*Open by appointment only.* Admission free.
Guided tours, lectures.
&#x267F; No access
&#x2740; Whitton

---

## Royal Naval College

King William Walk, Greenwich SE10. 081-858 2154.

A beautiful baroque masterpiece on the site of old Greenwich Palace, the Royal Naval College was originally built by Sir Christopher Wren as a hospital for naval pensioners. Two parts are open to the public: the large and richly decorated Chapel, rebuilt after a fire in 1779 to designs by James Stewart; and the amazing Painted Hall, the dining hall of the college. Decorative paintings, including *trompe l'oeils* of battle trophies, cover every inch of the walls, while an allegorical painting of William III and Queen Mary handing Liberty and Peace to Europe amidst swirling clouds and naked putti completely fills the vast ceiling. Starting in 1708, it took Sir James Thornhill 18 years to complete this work, which is surpassed only by the ceiling of the Sistine Chapel.

---

**Royal Naval College**
*Open 14.30-17.00 Mon-Wed & Fri-Sun.* Admission free.
⟨⟩ No access
⇷ Greenwich

---

## Rugby Football Museum

Rugby Football Union, Twickenham, Middlesex.
081-892 8161.

Containing sundry sporting relics such as balls, caps, ties, pictures, historic documents and other rugby memorabilia, the small museum at Twickenham is actually just the last part of a 1¼-hour guided tour which takes you behind the scenes of the much-revered home of rugby football. Starting with a short film on the tense build-up to an international, the tour takes you through the players' tunnel and up to the Royal Box, down into the medical, changing and bath rooms, on to the committee rooms to see pictures and trophies presented by other rugby unions from around the world, and finally to the museum where the tour ends. Here you can find out how the game has developed since first played at Rugby School over 150 years ago and how the Rugby Football Union itself was founded.

---

**Rugby Football Museum**
*Open for guided tours starting at 10.30 and 14.15 Mon-Fri, phone first to confirm availability.* Admission charge.
Guided tours. Guidebook.
*Educational facilities*: Tours for schools.
⟨⟩ Full access. Toilet.
⇷ Twickenham

---

## St Bride's Crypt Exhibition

St Bride's Church, Fleet Street EC4. 071-353 1301.     5 B2

Traditionally associated with the printers, writers and journalists of neighbouring Fleet Street, St Bride's is an historic church with its roots deep in London's past. The medieval church was destroyed in the Great Fire of 1666, and Wren's reconstruction (1671-75) suffered severe bomb damage in World War II. Before it was rebuilt after the war, the foundations were excavated and the archaeological remains, including a Roman pavement of about AD 180, put on show in the crypt, together with an exhibition about the history of the church, Fleet Street, and some of the characters connected with it: Wynkyn de Worde, Dr Johnson, Samuel Richardson, Ben Franklin and John Wilkes.

---

**St Bride's Crypt Exhibition**
*Open 09.00-17.00 Mon-Sun.* Admission free.
Shop. Guided tours. Guidebook.
*Educational facilities*: Tours for schools, lectures.
&#x267F; No access
&#x2296; Blackfriars

---

## St Paul's Cathedral Crypt and Treasury

St Paul's Cathedral EC4. 071-248 2705.     5 D2

The crypt of St Paul's, otherwise full of monuments and tombs, including those of the Duke of Wellington (1769-1852), Admiral Lord Nelson (1758-1805) and the cathedral's architect Sir Christopher Wren (1632-1723), contains an exhibition about the building of the cathedral following the destruction of its medieval predecessor during the Great Fire of 1666. The exhibition's centrepiece is the huge model Wren commissioned in 1674 to show what his proposed design would look like (this design was not the one eventually used when building work started the following year). Nearby you can see Wren's death mask and personal possessions such as his penknife, and, in the Cathedral treasury, post-Reformation plate and vestments from St Paul's and other churches within the Diocese of London.

---

**St Paul's Cathedral Crypt and Treasury**
*Open 09.30-16.25 Mon-Fri, 11.00-16.25 Sat.* Admission charge.
Shop. Guided tours. Guidebook.
*Educational facilities*: Tours for schools, lectures.
&#x267F; Full access. Toilet.
&#x2296; St Paul's

---

## Salvation Army International Heritage Centre

117-121 Judd Street WC1. 071-387 1656.

Opened in 1988, this modern exhibition on the third floor of a Salvation Army building focuses on the early history of the organisation and its founder, General William Booth, who died in 1912. Twenty-five numbered display cases, packed with all kinds of Sally Army exhibits and memorabilia, tell the story of Booth, a pawnbroker's apprentice turned preacher from Nottingham, and explain how his East London Christian Mission, founded in 1865, developed into the semi-military Salvation Army in 1878. The exhibition also covers the spread of the movement overseas, starting with Australia and the USA in 1880.

---

**Salvation Army International Heritage Centre**
*Open 09.30-15.30 Mon-Fri, 09.30-12.30 Sat.* Admission free.
Shop. Guided tours. Research facilities.
*Refreshments*: Café serving snacks and light meals *09.30-14.30*,
and hot lunches *11.30-13.15*.
*Educational facilities*: Tours for schools.
&#9855; Full access. Toilet.
&#10008; King's Cross

---

## Science Museum

Exhibition Road SW7. 071-938 8000.

The Science Museum is part of a countrywide network of institutions which together make up the national museum of science and industry. Broadly speaking, the Science Museum here in South Kensington, one of the three great national museums in the area, covers science, technology and medicine. It includes many historic exhibits, such as the 14thC clock from Wells Cathedral, as well as more modern ones, like the command module of the Apollo 10 spacecraft. Ranging in size from a tiny tea-making machine of 1904 to huge aircraft and steam locomotives, these show how modern scientific and industrial man has emerged, particularly over the last two centuries. The large number of inventions originating in this country helps explain in a practical way how, through technology, Britain became the dominant world power of the 19thC.

   Although the museum has a history going back nearly 150 years and has been on this site for nearly a century, it is very up-to-date both in terms of its contents and how it shows them. Younger visitors will be interested to know that, this being a practical museum, there are plenty of hands-on exhibits and interactive displays, especially in the Flight Lab near the Aeronautics Gallery (third floor), and in the Launch Pad (first floor), where you can use all sorts of puzzles and experiments to explore the basic principles behind everyday technology. There are also some really excellent sets showing things in context (a Victorian kitchen, for example, and a 1710 printer's shop); many reconstructions, some full-size (an iron and steel furnace and a nuclear reactor); and regular demonstrations of working objects (engines in the Power Gallery for example). To find out what's on when, ask at the Information Desk in the East Hall.

With more than 10,000 exhibits set out in over 40 galleries on 7 floors, the museum contains far too much for one visit.

*Mill Engine, Science Museum*

# Science Museum

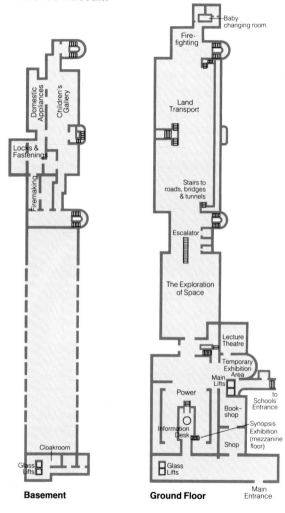

**Basement**

- Domestic Appliances
- Children's Gallery
- Locks & Fastenings
- Firemaking
- Cloakroom
- Glass Lifts

**Ground Floor**

- Baby changing room
- Fire-fighting
- Land Transport
- Stairs to roads, bridges & tunnels
- Escalator
- The Exploration of Space
- Lecture Theatre
- Temporary Exhibition Area
- Main Lifts
- to Schools' Entrance
- Power
- Book-shop
- Information Desk
- Synopsis Exhibition (mezzanine floor)
- Shop
- Glass Lifts
- Main Entrance

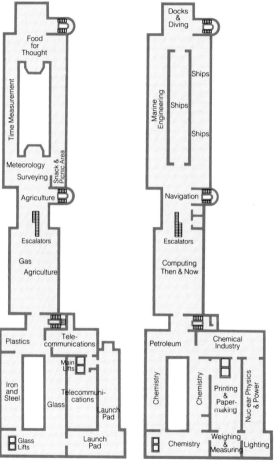

**First Floor**

**Second Floor**

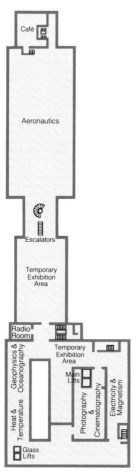

**Third Floor**

Café

Aeronautics

Escalators

Temporary Exhibition Area

Radio Room

Geophysics & Oceanography

Temporary Exhibition Area

Main Lifts

Heat & Temperature

Photography & Cinematography

Electricity & Magnetism

Glass Lifts

Main Lifts

Glimpses of Medical History

**Fourth Floor**

Veterinary History

Main Lifts

The Science & Art of Medicine

**Fifth Floor**

We recommend you choose a place to start from the floor plans above, or go to the Synopsis Exhibition on the ground floor which provides a very useful visual introduction to the museum and its contents. Basically the ground and floors 1-3 are the biggest, followed by the basement and then the relatively small 4th and 5th floors. The latter two house the Wellcome Museum of the History of Medicine, donated by Sir Henry Wellcome in 1977.

Once launched on your tour, there are 'explainers' in the Launch Pad (first floor) to answer questions. Elsewhere, from *11.15-13.30* and from *13.45-14.45*, suitably-dressed 'actor-interpreters' deal with queries as well as livening up the atmosphere a bit.

Below are listed some of the highlights:

### Basement

*Domestic Appliances*
A reconstruction of a Victorian kitchen
A 1904 tea-making machine

### Ground Floor

The Boulton and Watt steam engine of 1788
Arkwright's 1775 spinning machine
Foucault's pendulum showing that the earth rotates
*The Exploration of Space*
1969 Apollo 10 command module
Anders' space suit
*Land Transport*
The oldest original Rolls Royce (1905)
Stephenson's Rocket (1829)
Puffing Billy (1813), a railway locomotive

### First Floor

*Launch pad*
A hands-on gallery full of demonstration, experiments and puzzles where the principles behind modern technology can be explored.
*Iron and steel*
A mock-up of an open hearth furnace
*Telecommunications*
The first electric telegraph (1837)
*Agriculture*
Bell's reaper, the first machine for cutting corn (1826)
*Food for Thought*
A 1920s Sainsbury store

*Second Floor*
*Printing and paper-making*
A 1710 printer's shop
*Nuclear physics and power*
A life-sized reconstruction of part of a nuclear reactor

*Third Floor*

*Optics*
Hologram of Dennis Gabor, inventor of holograms
*Aeronautics*
Find out about the principles of flight with 24 hands-on exhibits. Hangar-like gallery displaying over 20 aircraft suspended from the roof, including a Spitfire, a Hurricane and Alcock and Brown's Vickers *Vimy*, the first aircraft to fly the Atlantic non-stop, in 1919.

*Fourth and Fifth Floors*

All 43 exhibits are either full-scale reconstructions or detailed models – covering human history between the neolithic age and the 1980s
*Glimpses of Medical History*
A 1930s dentist's chair
Childbirth in the 1860s
An open heart operation in 1980
Lister's Ward in 1868
*The Science and Art of Medicine*
Pasteur's equipment
1920s heart-lung apparatus

---

**Science Museum**
*Open 10.00-18.00 Mon-Sat, 11.00-18.00 Sun.* Admission charge.
Shop. Guidebook. Films. Research facilities.
*Refreshments*: Licensed restaurant serving hot meals and sandwiches, café serving drinks and snacks.
*Educational facilities*: Tours for schools, worksheets, lectures, workshops, activity area.
🅰 Full access. Toilet.
⊖ South Kensington

---

## Shakespeare Globe Museum
Bear Gardens, Bankside SE1. 071-620 0202.          5 D4
In Tudor times Londoners flocked over the river from the City to sample the taverns, brothels, theatres and animal-baiting rings of Bankside. Bear Gardens was the site of the bear-baiting arena. Here, in an old Georgian warehouse, the small Shakespeare Globe Museum tells the story of 'naughty' Bankside, how it came to be the red-light district of Tudor

London, and how the four theatres built here – including the Rose and Shakespeare's own theatre, the Globe – fitted into the overall picture of Elizabethan theatre-going. There are enlarged maps and pictures of the period, and excellent scale models of the theatres. Upstairs, you can see a replica of a 17thC indoor playhouse, occasionally used for real productions.

As well as the main display, the museum also contains exhibitions about the recently-discovered remains of the Globe and the Rose theatres. Among the finds is a bear's skull! In a room to one side there is another exhibition, with video, this time about the International Shakespeare Globe Centre's plans to build a reconstruction of Shakespeare's Globe on a riverside site close to the museum. Building has already started and it was originally planned to open the new theatre on Shakespeare's birthday, 23 April, in 1993. However, this would now seem less likely as progress is slow due to lack of funds.

---

**Shakespeare Globe Museum**
*Open 10.00-17.00 Mon-Sat, 14.00-17.30 Sun.* Admission charge.
Shop. Guided tours. Guidebook. Films.
*Educational facilities:* Tours for schools, worksheets, lectures, workshops.
🚻 Full access to museum; no access to theatre. Toilet.
⊖ Cannon Street, London Bridge

---

## Silver Studio Collection
Middlesex Polytechnic, Bounds Green Road, New Southgate N11. 081-368 1299 x 7339.
Established in 1880, the Silver Studio was the leading independent commercial studio of its day. The designs it sold were mainly for textiles, wallpapers and floor coverings, but silverware, graphics, and ceramics also came within its range. Its clients were manufacturers and famous retailers like Liberty. After the studio closed in 1963, all its designs and records were presented to Hornsey College of Art, now part of Middlesex Polytechnic. The collection is an excellent resource for the study of decorative design from the 1880s onwards and can be seen in a special room created out of the proceeds of licensing agreements.

---

**Silver Studio Collection**
*Open by appointment 10.00-16.00 Mon-Fri.* Admission free.
Guidebook. Research facilities.
🚻 Full access. Toilet.
⊖ Bounds Green

---

## Story of Telecommunications

145 Queen Victoria Street EC4. 071-248 7444.            5 D3

The Story of Telecommunications is British Telecom's very own museum and is the only one of its kind in the country. On two levels, the entrance level chronicles the rise of telecommunications from the invention of the telegraph in the early 19thC, through the development of the telephone, to the age of digital transmission and the fax. The lower level looks in more detail at the development of the telecommunications system in the UK, and at technical features of telephones and telegraphs. It is a modern display, full of flashing lights and the sounds of clicking switchgear, ringing phones and video soundtracks – children love it!

The museum contains many early telegraphs (though not the first, which is in the Science Museum) and just about every model of telephone produced in the UK before the recent deregulation, including a splendid example used in the Rothschilds' London home in the 20s. There are also exchange machines of various kinds, and modern equipment like telexes, faxes and computers, all of which can be used.

Other exhibits include network maps and photographs, examples of early telegrams and telephone company advertising, and various other historical exhibits, such as a section of the first submarine cable linking Britain with Belgium. One of the most unusual displays describes the Electrophone. At the beginning of this century subscribers to this special service could listen to live plays and concerts on their telephones in the comfort of their own home. Of course, radio broadcasting soon killed the service off but it was very popular in its day.

---

**Story of Telecommunications**
*Open 10.00-17.00 Mon-Fri. Closed Bank Hols.* Admission free.
Shop. Guided tours. Guidebook. Films. Research facilities.
*Educational facilities*: Tours for schools, worksheets, lectures, workshops.
&#9855; Full access. Toilet.
&#9758; Blackfriars

---

## Tea & Coffee Museum

The Clove Building, Maguire Street SE1.            5 G4
071-378 0222.

Situated on the South Bank at Butler's Wharf, this charming, unusual museum houses the Bramah Collection of tea and coffee exhibits, including many rare items. There are silver and ceramic teapots, teaware and coffee-making equipment from all over the world. The collection also has over 200 prints, paintings and photographs relating to the history of tea from between 1740 and 1840. It includes works by (or after) Banbury, Nixon, Heath, Isaac and George Cruikshank, Rowlandson and Gillray. Of course, after perusing the collection, you can be refreshed by *good* coffee and tea in the coffee bar and tea room!

---

**Tea & Coffee Museum**
*Open 10.00-18.00 Mon-Sat, 14.00-18.00 Sun.* Admission charge.
Shop. Guided tours.
*Refreshments*: Tea and coffee in the tea room and coffee bar.
*Educational facilities*: Tours for schools.
&#9855; Full access. Toilet.
&#9960; London Bridge

---

### Theatre Museum
Russell Street WC2. 071-836 7891.                                4 F3

An outpost of the Victorian and Albert Museum, this national museum of the performing arts is very appropriately located in Covent Garden – the historic heart of London's theatreland. It covers all aspects of professional live entertainment, from theatre, opera and ballet to magic, mime, rock and pop, circus and variety, pantomime and music hall. Opened in 1987 after nearly a century of private collecting, fund-raising and lobbying, it is based in the old Covent Garden flower market which it shares with the London Transport Museum.

Descending from the ground-floor entrance to the basement level display areas, you pass by walls covered with signed, coloured handprints of famous performers – a tradition of the museum. At the bottom, on the right, is the museum's picture gallery. Done out like the foyer of an Edwardian theatre, it contains the largest exhibition of theatrical paintings on public display in Britain. Three centuries of actors and actresses can be seen here, including Killigrew and Garrick from the 18thC and John Gielgud and Herbert Lom from our own day.

The main display gallery takes the form of a theatrically-lit passage round four sides of a square. Set into the walls are display areas and cabinets of different sizes filled with all manner of theatrical treasures from the museum's vast collection. Arranged in chronological order to show how the British stage has developed from the age of Shakespeare to the present day, they include model theatres and sets, programmes, tickets and souvenirs, make-up, props and costumes, plus personal possessions of famous people connected with the stage such as Mick Jagger's 1972 stage suit and a pair of boots once worn by the greatest tragic actress of the Georgian stage, Sarah Siddons (1755-1831).

*Theatre Museum*

Thousands more illustrations and documents from the museum's collections are mounted on pull-out cases in the Beard Room next door to the main gallery. These are useful if you want to explore individual theatrical subjects like alternative comedy or lost theatres in more detail. Another feature of the museum is the studio theatre, which specialises in new or experimental work. Evening performances start shortly after the museum closes so you could easily combine a museum visit with a night out at the theatre, particularly as tickets to West End shows are on sale in the box office.

---

**Theatre Museum**
*Open 11.00-19.00 Tue-Sun.* Admission charge.
Shop. Guided tours. Guidebook. Films. Research facilities.
*Refreshments*: Café (licensed) serving light meals and snacks
*11.00-19.00 Tue-Sun.*
*Educational facilities*: Tours, worksheets, lectures, workshops.
&#9855; Full access. Toilet.
&#1012; Covent Garden

---

## Tower Bridge Museum
Tower Bridge SE1. 071-407 0922.
Tower Bridge still works, but by electricity rather than steam. The conversion in 1976 means that visitors are now able to see the inner workings of one of the great masterpieces of Victorian engineering.

The two stone-clad, steel-framed towers – linked by an overhead walkway which gives amazing panoramic views up and down the river, contain excellent displays on London's docklands, on other bridges across the Thames within the City boundaries, and, of course, on the history of Tower Bridge itself. Designed by Sir Horace Jones and Sir John Wolfe Barry, the new bridge opened in 1894 giving London the extra road crossing it badly needed, while at the same time allowing tall ships to continue to sail on upstream into the Pool of London just below London Bridge.

Underneath the approach road at the southern end of the bridge you see the huge boilers and gleaming engines (one in motion) which provided the hydraulic power to lift one of the 1200-ton arms (an identical engine room at the north end of the bridge lifted the other arm, or bascule as it is called). Amazingly, the engine never failed in all their 80-odd years of service. Right at the end of the tour a video and model show clearly how the lift mechanism works. Unfortunately, you

*Tower Bridge*

cannot actually see this part of the bridge because it is still in operation (the bascules are raised about five times a week to allow shipping through).

---

**Tower Bridge Museum**
*Open Apr-Oct 10.00-18.30 Mon-Sun; Nov-Mar 10.00-16.45 Mon-Sun.* Admission charge.
Shop. Guided tours.
*Educational facilities*: Tours for schools, worksheets.
&#x267F; Full access. Toilet.
&#x2296; Tower Hill

---

## Tower Hill Pageant
1 Tower Hill Terrace EC3. 071-709 0081.
One of London's newest attractions, the Tower Hill Pageant is the city's first so-called 'dark ride' museum. Having descended to the bottom level of converted wine vaults near the Tower of London, you step into an automated car for a brief 15-minute journey past a series of tableaux depicting scenes from 2000 years of London history. The Pageant focuses on the riverside port area and shows scenes from Roman and Saxon times, a medieval merchant in his quayside warehouse, Londoners fleeing in panic before the Great Fire of 1066, a Georgian coffee-house, the great warehouses of the 19thC port, and the view from German bombers as they blitzed the docks in 1940. To add atmosphere, many of the models – like the medieval lout who lurches out of a doorway – move, while others speak in strange tongues like Anglo-Saxon. Piped odours, like the acrid smell of London burning in the Great Fire, also help to make the whole experience that little bit more authentic.

The Pageant is based on excavations along the Thames waterfront by Museum of London archaeologists and incorporates hundreds of their Roman, Saxon and medieval finds. Many more are on show in the Pageant's museum of waterfront archaeology on the level above the dark ride.

---

**Tower Hill Pageant**
*Open Apr-Sep 09.30-17.30 Mon-Sun; Nov-Mar 09.30-16.30 Mon-Sun.* Admission charge.
Shop. Guidebook.
*Educational facilities*: Worksheets.
&#x267F; Full access. Toilet.
&#x2296; Tower Hill

### Tower of London

Tower Hill EC3. 071-709 0765.

Begun by William the Conqueror in the 11thC, the Tower of London is a medieval royal fortress with a large central keep encircled by two rings of walls. It's so big that there are streets and houses inside, some providing homes for the Yeoman Warders who surpervise the opening of the Tower to the public. They are much in evidence in their spectacular Tudor uniforms, blue in winter, and red in summer. The Tower's other inhabitants are, of course, the famous black ravens.

*Tower of London*

When you go to the Tower there are four main things to see: the Tower itself, the Royal Armouries collection, the Crown Jewels and the museum of the Royal Regiment of Fusiliers (for which there is a small additional charge).

In its 950-year history the Tower has been many things – from mint and menagerie to palace and treasury – but it is best known as a prison, and a place of torture and execution. On your tour you will see Traitor's Gate where prisoners were brought into the Tower by river; the headsman's axe and block; one of the actual places of execution near the castle chapel; and several of the thick-walled towers in which prisoners were kept. In Bloody Tower the Little Princes were smothered in 1483. A century later Sir Walter Ralegh was a prisoner here and two rooms have been furnished to show how a well-born prisoner like him probably lived.

The quite stupendous Royal Armouries collection is the largest and most valuable of its kind in the world. There are hundreds of suits and pieces of armour and thousands of weapons dating from the Middle Ages to the 19thC and coming from Japan, India, Africa and Turkey as well as Britain, Europe and America. Some of the highlights are Henry VIII's armour and tilting lances; Wild West guns, including the Winchester repeater; and a huge suit of elephant armour said to have been captured by Robert Clive at the Battle of Plassey in India in 1757. Most of the armour and weapons are in the central keep or White Tower (where also, incidentally, you can see the austerely beautiful Norman chapel of St John – the oldest in London).

The Waterloo Block houses the Tower's most valuable collection: the Crown Jewels. These include the Star of Africa – the largest cut diamond in the world. All the most precious items – crowns, orbs, sceptres and other regalia encrusted with precious stones – are in the dimly-lit steel vault deep in the basement. On the ground floor, in show cases, you can see great gilt wine coolers and flagons, maces, swords, orders, trumpets and the sovereign's coronation robes.

Finally, the Tower is also home to the museum of the Royal Regiment of Fusiliers. Three small rooms packed with displays and regimental relics tell the story of the regiment from its foundation in 1685 up to the present day. The regiment was created specifically to protect the Royal guns kept within the Tower, and its name comes from the improved musket or 'fusil' with which the first recruits were armed. One of these fusils is in the museum, along with many other weapons, uniforms, pictures and personal possessions of officers and men.

---

**Tower of London**
*Open Mar-Oct 09.30-18.30 Mon-Sat, 14.00-17.00 Sun; Nov-Feb 09.30-17.00 Mon-Sat.* Admission charge.
Shop. Guided tours. Guidebook. Films. Research facilities.
*Educational facilities*: Tours for schools, worksheets, lectures.
🚲 Partial access. Toilet.
⊖ Tower Hill

---

## Twinings in the Strand

216 The Strand WC2. 071-353 3511.     4 F3

Thomas Twining founded his famous tea business in 1706 and Twinings have been here on this site in the Strand ever since. The doorway, topped with figures of Chinese mandarins, was made in 1787. As you walk through the narrow shop (formerly an alleyway), you see pictures of Thomas, his family and descendants. In the room at the back, the actual site of the original Twinings office, there is a small collection relating to the history of the firm and the family: books from the archives, 18thC invoices, tea bricks, 18thC and 19thC English and Chinese tea caddies, price lists and brochures, prints, photographs and family trees. The business is still family-run.

---

**Twinings in the Strand**
*Open 09.30-16.00 Mon-Fri, subject to the museum room not being used for company meetings. Phone for details.* Admission free.
Shop.
🚲 No access
⊖ Charing Cross

---

## University College London

Gower Street WC1. 071-387 7050.     1 F5

Founded in 1826, University College London is the oldest part of London University. The **College Exhibition**, in the north cloisters, tells the story of the founding of the College and features some of the famous people who have been staff and students. In the south cloisters you can see the figure of the philosopher Jeremy Bentham (died 1832) whose ideas inspired the College's founders (the figure is actually his skeleton covered by his original clothes and his wax death mask).

The **Strang Print Room** contains the University's collection of prints and drawings, including old master etchings, engravings and early English mezzotints. Also on display are Turner's *Liber Studiorum* and drawings by the famous sculptor Flaxman, plus many German drawings of the 16thC-18thC. The Slade Collection, with works by teachers, students and prizewinners, illustrates the history of the Slade School of Art from the late 19thC. Plaster models made by Flaxman for his marble church monuments are in the adjacent neo-classical **Flaxman Gallery**, beneath the dome of the central building of the college.

The **Petrie Museum of Egyptian Archaeology** contains a large collection of Egyptian antiquities assembled over a century of excavations by London University archaeologists, beginning in the 1880s with the famous Egyptologist, W.M. Flinders Petrie. It is an academic collection used mainly for teaching and research.

The **Museum of Zoology and Comparative Anatomy** covers the whole of the Animal Kingdom and is another academic collection primarily used for teaching. It was started in 1828 by Robert Grant, the first ever professor of the subject in England.

---

**College Exhibition and Flaxman Gallery**
*Open 10.00-17.00 Mon-Fri. Closed Bank Hols and for one week at both Christmas and Easter.* Admission free.
&#9855; Full access. Toilet.
&#9719; Euston Square

**Strang Print Room**
*Open during term time 13.00-14.15 Mon-Fri. Reserve collections by appointment 13.00-16.00 during term time.* Admission free.
Guidebook.
&#9855; Full access. Toilet.
&#9719; Euston Square

**Petrie Museum of Egyptian Archaeology**
*Open 10.00-12.00 & 13.15-17.00 Mon-Fri. Closed for one week at both Christmas and Easter, and mid Aug-mid Sep.* Admission free.
Guided tours.
*Educational facilities*: Tours for schools, lectures, workshops.
&#9855; Partial access. Toilet.
&#9719; Euston Square

**Museum of Zoology and Comparative Anatomy**
*Open 10.30-17.00 Mon-Fri. Closed Bank Hols and for one week at both Christmas and Easter.* Admission free.
Shop.
&#9855; Full access. Toilet.
&#9719; Euston Square

**Victoria & Albert Museum**
Cromwell Road SW7. 071-938 8500.
The Victoria & Albert Museum is Britain's national museum
of art and design and the largest one of its kind in the world.
Illustrating thousands of years of creative output from all
parts of the globe, its huge collection of over a million objects
is drawn from fields as varied as ceramics, furniture, jewellery, metalwork, textiles, dress, painting, sculpture, silver
and interior design (some of the exhibits are period rooms

*Victoria & Albert Museum*

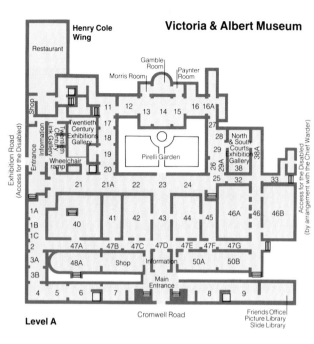

**Level A**

## Art and design galleries

1-7 Europe 1600-1800
8 Europe & America 1800-1890
9 Europe & America 1890-1900
12-20 Italy 1400-1500
21-22 Europe 1500-1600
23-24 Europe 1100-1450
25 Spain 1450-1550
26-29A Northern Europe 1450-1550
32-33 Tapestry, maps and carpets
40 Dress, Europe 1600-present
41 The Nehuru Gallery of Indian Art 1550-1990
42 Art of the Islamic World 700-1800
43 Medieval Treasury Europe 400-1400
44 The T. T. Tsui Gallery of Chinese Art
45 The Toshiba Gallery of Japanese Art
46A Plaster casts, Northern Europe
46 Fakes and forgeries
46B Plaster casts, Italy
47A-47E Indian sculpture
47F China export art
47G Plaster casts
48A Raphael Cartoons
50A-50B Sculpture & Architecture, Britain

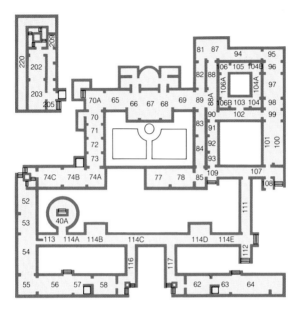

**Level B**

40A  Musical instruments
52-57  Britain 1500-1715
58  Britain 1715-1750
62-64  Sculpture and carvings
65-73  Silver
74A-C  Britain 1900-1960
77-78  National Art Library
81-82 & 89  Metalwork
83-85  Church Plate
88-88A  Arms and armour
91-93  Jewellery
94  Tapestries
95-101 & 107-109  Textiles
102  Costume jewellery
103-106B  20th Century design
111  Stained & engraved glass
112  Glass, modern
113-114E  Ironwork
116-117  Stained glass
202-203  Cole Exhibition gallery
205 & 209  Printmaking techniques
220  European ornaments gallery

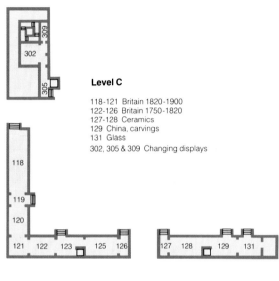

**Level C**

118-121 Britain 1820-1900
122-126 Britain 1750-1820
127-128 Ceramics
129 China, carvings
131 Glass
302, 305 & 309 Changing displays

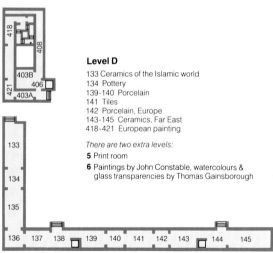

**Level D**

133 Ceramics of the Islamic world
134 Pottery
139-140 Porcelain
141 Tiles
142 Porcelain, Europe
143-145 Ceramics, Far East
418-421 European painting

*There are two extra levels:*

**5** Print room
**6** Paintings by John Constable, watercolours &
glass transparencies by Thomas Gainsborough

lifted out of demolished mansions). Several individual sections of foreign art – Japanese lacquer, Renaissance Italian sculpture, Indian art – are the best anywhere in the world outside their country of origin. Lovers of British paintings should note that, thanks to the generosity of the artist's daughter, the V & A also houses the world's largest collection of Constable paintings.

The brainchild of Prince Albert, husband of Queen Victoria, the museum was founded as the Museum of Manufactures in 1852 to promote the influence of art and design in manufacturing industry. This had been one of the chief aims of the Great Exhibition held the year before. The proceeds from this hugely successful exhibition were used to buy the land for the V & A and the other great national museums nearby (the Science Museum and the Natural History Museum).

There are two main sections to the museum: the main building, facing Cromwell Road; and the much smaller Henry Cole Wing, facing Exhibition Road, on whose restored Great Staircase (recently opened to the public) hang over 300 paintings arranged in order of artistic hierarchy prescribed by Sir Joshua Reynolds. Inside the main building, the 150-odd rooms (totalling 7 miles (11km) in length!) fall into two main types. It is worth being aware of these before you begin your tour. The **Art and Design Galleries** show objects made in the same place or roughly at the same time. These are mostly on the ground floor (Level A). The **Materials and Techniques Galleries**, mostly on the first floor (Level B) and above, present objects grouped together by type – ceramics, textiles and jewellery for example. A notable exception is the Dress Collection (400 years of European fashion) which is on Level A.

Below are listed some of the main highlights with room numbers:

### Level A
41   – Tipoo's Tiger - life-sized 18thC automaton captured
         from the Sultan of Mysore in 1799
46B – Reproduction of Michelangelo's David
48A– Raphael Cartoons - designs for Sistine Chapel
         tapestries painted about 1515 and among the finest
         surviving examples of Italian Renaissance art

### Level B
54   – Great Bed of Ware – huge carved four-poster made in
         England about 1590

58  –  Norfolk House Music Room – mid-18thC Rococo
        interior from a nobleman's house in St James's Square
        in London
94  –  Devonshire Hunting Tapestries – huge, colourful
        tapestries once owned by the Dukes of Devonshire
        showing courtly hunts in the 15thC

---

**Victoria & Albert Museum**
*Open 10.00-17.50 Mon-Sat, 14.30-17.50 Sun.* Admission free, but
donations invited on entry.
Shop. Guided tours. Guidebook. Films. Research facilities.
*Refreshments*: The New Restaurant, serving excellent hot & cold
buffet lunches *11.00-14.00 Mon-Sat*; home-made cakes and
sandwiches *10.00-17.00 Mon-Sat, 14.30-17.30 Sun.* Café 38 coffee
shop serving drinks, sandwiches and pastries *10.30-17.00 Mon-Sat,
14.30-17.00 Sun.*
*Educational facilities*: Tours for schools, worksheets, lectures, workshops.
&#9855; Partial access. Toilet.
&#8854; South Kensington

---

## Vintage Wireless Museum
23 Rosendale Road, Dulwich SE21. 081-670 3667.
Radio enthusiast Gerald Wells started what has become
Britain's largest wireless museum in 1964, and keeps it in the
large Victorian house in south London where he has lived all
his life. Having long-since spilled out into specially-designed
outbuildings, it contains thousands of vintage wirelesses, most
of them in working order, plus many old TVs and a huge
collection of spare parts. Wells draws on the latter to repair
and maintain radios in the collection or brought in by fellow
members of the British Vintage Wireless Society (of which
his house is the HQ), and to make reproduction vintage
wirelesses for sale. A must for anyone with a nostalgic or
technical interest in the early days of radio broadcasting.

---

**Vintage Wireless Museum**
*Open by appointment only.* Admission free.
Guided tours. Guidebook. Research facilities.
&#9855; Partial access
&#8658; Tulse Hill, West Dulwich

---

## Westminster Abbey Museum
Westminster Abbey, Broad Sanctuary SW1.                  4 F6
071-222 5152.
The Abbey Museum is housed in the vaulted stone undercroft
of what was the monks' dormitory. It was built nearly a

thousand years ago and is reached through the Abbey cloisters. The main exhibits are amazing royal and noble funeral effigies dating from medieval times to the early 19thC. In the beginning these effigies were borne on coffins. Later they were made to stand at the place of burial. For many early ones, only the heads survive, that of Henry VII, based on a death mask, is really lifelike and arresting. The later and more sophisticated ones have wax faces and are fully dressed in original costume. There is a particularly nice one of Admiral Lord Nelson in full uniform standing in a relaxed pose. Charles II, with his pencil moustache, was said by a contemporary to be a great likeness.

Other exhibits include General Monck's armour; shields, swords, a saddle and a helmet carried at the funerals of those two stout warriors Edward III and Henry V; and replica crown jewels used in coronation rehearsals. There are also small displays on royal funerals and coronations, and on the history of the Abbey.

Included in the museum ticket are the Pyx Chamber and the Chapter House. The Pyx Chamber was originally used for testing coins of the realm. Now it contains plate from the Abbey and neighbouring St Margaret's church. The beautiful Chapter House, with its medieval wall paintings and tiled floor, was the monks' assembly room. It was also, incidentally, the meeting place of Henry III's Great Council, and is there-fore a precursor of our modern Houses of Parliament.

---

**Westminster Abbey Museum**
*10.30-16.00 Mon-Sun.* Admission charge.
Shop. Guidebook. Research facilities.
*Educational facilities*: Tours for schools, lectures.
&#x267F; Partial access
&#x2296; Westminster

---

## Wimbledon Lawn Tennis Museum

All England Club, Church Road, Wimbledon SW19.
081-946 6131.
Most people only go to Wimbledon when the championships are on, but it is also well worth making a trip at quieter times of the year to visit the special tennis museum there. At least it's one way of getting to see Centre Court! You will also find out about the history of the game, watch films of great players – past and present – in action, and see some of their personal possessions and other memorabilia, such as the match clothes of Martina Navratilova and Bjorn Borg. Two recent innova-tions in the museum are an interactive computer system which

allows you to summon up up-to-date information on the players, tennis history and the Championships; and an educational computer tennis game complete with talking umpire.

---

**Wimbledon Lawn Tennis Museum**
*Open 11.00-17.00 Tue-Sat, 14.00-17.00 Sun. Closed Bank Hols,*
*Fri-Sun prior to Championships, and middle Sun of Championships.*
Admission charge.
Shop. Films. Research facilities.
&#x267f; Full access. Toilet.
&#x2296; Southfields

---

## Wimbledon Windmill Museum

Windmill Road, Wimbledon Common SW19.
081-788 7655/081-947 2825.
Wimbledon Windmill was built at the northern end of Wimbledon Common in 1817 and worked up until the 1860s. Today, a small museum on the first floor tells the story of windmills and windmilling in pictures, models and the machinery and tools of the trade. The museum also contains a large collection of woodworking tools.

---

**Wimbledon Windmill Museum**
*Open Apr-Oct 14.00-17.00 Sat, Sun and Bank hols.* Admission charge.
Shop. Guided tours. Guidebook. Films.
*Refreshments*: Café serving snacks and hot & cold meals.
*Educational facilities*: Tours for schools, worksheets, lectures, workshops.
&#x267f; No access
&#x2296; Wimbledon (then bus 93)

---

*Wimbledon Windmill, Wimbledon Common*

# HISTORIC HOUSE MUSEUMS

## Boston Manor House

Boston Manor Road, Brentford, Middlesex. 081-570 0622 x 270.
A fine Jacobean mansion with remarkable plaster ceilings and
chimneypieces, Boston Manor was built in 1662 by a Lady
Reade, and shortly after passed to the Clitherow family. They
owned it until 1921 when it was bought by the local Council.
Today, most of the house is given over to flats for members of
the Over Forty Association of Women Workers, but the three
principal rooms on the first floor are open to the public. In
one, a small permanent exhibition tells the story of the house.
One of the other rooms normally has a second temporary
exhibition covering some aspect of the history of the area.
As yet the house contains no original furniture and only a
few pictures (one is a Kneller portrait of a member of
the Clitherow family), but there are plans to build up the
collections, funds permitting.

> **Boston Manor House**
> *Open end May-early Sep 14.00-16.30 Sun only.* Admission free.
> Guided tours.
> &#9855; No access
> &#9758; Boston Manor

## Carew Manor

Church Road, Beddington, Surrey. 081-642 8349.
Originally a medieval moated manor house, three separate
rebuildings – the most recent in 1866 – have done away with
most of its historic features. However, visitors can still see the
Great Hall with its 15thC hammerbeam roof, the medieval
cellars, and the early 18thC dovecote with over 1000 nesting
boxes. There is a display on the history of the house and the
Carew family who owned it for 400 years. The house is now a
school.

> **Carew Manor**
> *Open Sun & Bank Hols. Phone for times.* Admission charge.
> Guided tours. Guidebook.
> &#9855; No access
> &#8916; Wallington (then bus 403)

## Carlyle's House

24 Cheyne Row SW3. 071-352 7087.                    6 E4

A fine terraced house built in the early 18thC and made
famous as the home of Thomas Carlyle, the great 19thC writer
who became known as the Sage of Chelsea. Born in Scotland
in 1795, Carlyle moved here with his wife in 1834 and died in
the house, 15 years after his wife, in 1881. The house opened
as a museum in 1895 and was taken over by the National
Trust in 1936. Furnished in the period, it contains much of the
Carlyles' own furniture, books and pictures, as well as more
personal possessions like his walking stick and hat; the latter
hangs in the hall by the garden door.

Carlyle's reputation as a literary and intellectual giant
rested partly on his own personal gifts and partly on his
books, two of which were written here: *The French
Revolution*, written in the first-floor library, and *Frederick the
Great*, composed over 12 years in the special sound-proofed
attic study constructed at the top of the house.

Other rooms on show are the stone-flagged basement
kitchen where Carlyle had to go if he wanted to smoke a pipe
– Mrs Carlyle wouldn't have tobacco smoke in the house; the
ground-floor sitting-room, dining room, china closet and
entrance hall; and the first-floor bedroom and dressing room,
complete with Carlyle's own wash basin and hip bath.
Throughout the house there are photographs and pictures of
the Carlyles, the people and places associated with them, and
some fascinating interior views of the house as it looked when
the Carlyles were in residence.

---

**Carlyle's House**
*Open Apr-Oct 11.00-17.00 Wed-Sun & Bank Hols*. Admission
charge.
Guidebook.
*Educational facilities*: Tours for schools, lectures.
🚫 No access
⊖ South Kensington (then bus 45, 49, 219)

---

## Carshalton House

Pound Street, Carshalton, Surrey. 081-770 4746.

Carshalton House was built in 1707 by Edward Carleton
around the core of an older house. A later 18thC owner, probably Sir John Fellowes, Sub-Governor of the South Sea
Company, added the unique Water Tower in the grounds, a
plunge bath tiled with hand-painted blue delft. Today the
house is a convent school, but visitors are allowed in several

times a year to see the Water Tower and the principal rooms of the house; the Blue Room, the spectacular Painted Parlour and the 19thC chapel.

---
**Carlshalton House**
*Open about three times a year. Phone for details.* Admission charge.
Guided tours. Guidebook.
*Refreshments*: Drinks and snacks served in the house.
&#9855; Partial access
&#8812; Carshalton

---

## Charles Darwin Museum

Luxted Road, Downe, Orpington, Kent. (0689) 859119.
In this modest country house Charles Darwin spent the last 40 years of his sickness-ridden life. As well as the garden, five rooms and the hall are on show, furnished as they were in Darwin's time. The drawing room was the family's main living room. The New Study contains displays on the theory of evolution for which Darwin is famous. The Erasmus Darwin Room, with its collections of Wedgwood medallions and paintings by Joseph Wright of Derby, is concerned with Darwin's grandfather, Erasmus Darwin. He was a doctor in 18thC Lichfield with a modest literary reputation. But the two most important rooms are the Charles Darwin Room and the Old Study. The former contains many of Darwin's instruments, personal possessions and notes, and the priceless original manuscript of the diary he kept on his five-year voyage on the *Beagle* (1831-36). The latter was Darwin's cluttered study, where he did his experimental work and produced most of his books, including his most famous work, *The Origin of Species.*

---
**Charles Darwin Museum**
*Open 13.00-18.00 Wed-Sun & Bank Hols. Closed Feb and mid Dec-1 Jan.* Admission charge.
Shop. Guidebook.
&#9855; Full access
&#8812; Orpington (then bus R2), Bromley South (then bus 146)

---

## Chiswick House

Burlington Lane, Chiswick W4. 081-995 0508.
This is a remarkable country house set in famous landscaped gardens in west London. In designing it, its architect-owner, the Earl of Burlington, went back to the work of the 16thC Italian neo-classical architect Andrea Palladio and consc-

iously attempted to re-create the kind of villa you might have found in the suburbs of ancient Rome. Built in the 1720s before Palladio's ideas had really taken hold in England, Chiswick House is one of the earliest and purest examples of Palladianism, and one of the precursors of the Palladian craze that swept the country in the ensuing decades.

The house is relatively small and basically square, with an octagonal core on both floors. Throughout it is stone-floored and sparsely furnished, though the grander rooms on the first floor retain many of the paintings which hung in the house in Burlington's day. These rooms are also richly ornamented, with carved and gilded mouldings and, in some cases, painted ceilings. These are mainly the work of William Kent, though the ceiling painting in the Gallery – *The Relief of Smyrna* – is much older and thought to be the work of Veronese. The grandest room is the magnificent central Saloon or Tribunal, with its richly carved frieze and dome towering above the rest of the house. Classical busts on gilded brackets encircle the room beneath the eight large paintings, one for each face of the octagon.

The downstairs rooms, besides being low-ceilinged, are much plainer, with very little ornamentation and only a few chairs and paintings. In Burlington's day they were put to homely domestic uses. Now they are the scene of an exhibition (including audio-visuals) which tells the story of Lord Burlington and his extraordinary house.

Passages on both ground and first floors give access to the 'Link' building which once linked Chiswick House with an older house close by. Beneath the lower hall you can see the vaulted brick cellar full of beer barrels.

---

**Chiswick House**
*Open Good Fri or 1 Apr (whichever is earlier)-Sep 10.00-18.00 Mon-Sun. Oct-Maundy Thur or 31 Mar (whichever is earlier) 10.00-16.00 Mon-Sun.* Admission charge.
Shop.
*Refreshments*: Drinks and snacks served in house.
&#9855; Partial access
&#8804; Chiswick

---

## Church Farm House Museum
Greyhound Hill, Hendon NW4. 081-203 0130.
A 17thC farmhouse set in its own gardens close to St Mary's Church in Hendon. Downstairs you can see the panelled dining room furnished in the simple but handsome style of the

*Church Farm House Museum*

18thC. Close by is the remarkable stone-flagged kitchen with its period furniture and artefacts dating from the time when Church Farm was a family farm supplying hay for the London market. The chief feature of the kitchen is the huge fireplace – incorporating a bread oven, spit and chimney crane – decked out with various old-fashioned cooking pots and other kitchen utensils. Upstairs, the first-floor rooms are used for changing exhibitions, some of local and historical interest, others more general.

---

**Church Farm House**
*Open 10.00-13.00 & 14.00-17.30 Mon & Wed-Sat, 10.00-13.00 Tue, 14.00-17.30 Sun.* Admission free.
Guided tours. Guidebook.
*Educational facilities:* Tours for schools.
&#9855; No access
&#9784; Hendon Central

---

**Croydon Palace**

Old Palace Road, Croydon, Surrey. 081-680 5877.

Now a girls' school, Croydon Palace was used for centuries as a country residence by the Archbishops of Canterbury. On the guided tour you will see the 15thC Great Hall and guardroom, the chapel and Long Gallery, the Norman undercroft and the bedroom used by Queen Elizabeth I.

---

**Croydon Palace**

*Guided tours Easter, May & Jul. Phone for precise dates.* Tours leave *14.00-14.30.* Admission charge.

Guidebook.

*Refreshments*: Home-made tea served in the undercroft

♿ No access

⇌ West Croydon

---

**Dickens House Museum**

48 Doughty Street WC1. 071-405 2127.

This is the house a young Charles Dickens and family moved into in 1837 when the writer was just beginning to make a name for himself. It is a handsome Georgian terraced house in an equally handsome street, with three storeys, plus basement and attic, filled with furniture, pictures, books, manuscripts, letters, personal possessions and other relics associated with Dickens, his family and, of course, the hundreds of characters in his novels. The author's study, where he completed *The*

*Dickens House Museum*

*Pickwick Papers* and wrote most of *Oliver Twist* and *Nicholas Nickleby*, was probably the back room on the first floor, next to the drawing room. On the floor above are his sister-in-law's room and Dickens' own bedroom and dressing room where the Suzannet collection of Dickensiana is displayed. The Comte de Suzannet (1882-1950) was a great Dickens enthusiast, and his unique collection includes the velvet-covered desk and several books marked up with stage directions which Dickens used on his famous reading tours. On the ground floor is the family's dining room and informal sitting room. Below in the basement is the old kitchen, converted into a quiet library and sitting room for visitors, and the still room and wash house. These and other features make Dickens' House worth visiting as much for its period domestic interest as for the relics of the great writer it contains.

---

**Dickens House Museum**
*Open 10.00-17.00 Mon-Sat.* Admission charge.
Guidebook. Research facilities.
*Educational facilities*: Tours for schools.
⟁ Partial access
⊖ Russell Square

---

## Dr Johnson's House
17 Gough Square EC4. 071-353 3745.
An old house in a small courtyard off Fleet Street where 18thC writer, wit and critic Dr Samuel Johnson lived from 1748 to 1759. It was in the large attic at the top of the house that, with six assistants, he compiled the first comprehensive dictionary of the English language, so the place is an important literary shrine. It is also the only one of Johnson's many London homes to have survived, and has retained its relaxed homely atmosphere. One almost expects Johnson himself to walk in at any moment demanding a dish of tea.

When newspaper magnate Lord Harmsworth rescued the house from demolition earlier this century it was little more than a shell. Since then it has been completely restored, and besides a fine, contemporary, American pine staircase and many period features and pieces of furniture, it now contains portraits, letters, books and relics of Johnson and his circle to remind us of mid-Georgian London and the man who dominated its literary life for 30 years. Worth looking out for in particular are the copy of Johnson's Dictionary, his portrait by Sir Joshua Reynolds and a fine painting of his black servant Francis Barber.

> **Dr Johnson's House**
> *Open 11.00-17.30 Mon-Sat (to 17.00 Oct-Apr).* Admission charge.
> Shop.
> ♿ No access
> ⊖ Temple, Chancery Lane, Blackfriars

## Fenton House

Windmill Hill, Hampstead NW3. 071-435 3471.

A small country house built on a hilltop in Hampstead in 1693, it is not known for whom. It got its present name a century later when it was bought by Philip Fenton, a Baltic merchant. His son James made various internal alterations in the Regency style, though he kept much of the original panelling and the 17thC pine staircases. Little has been touched since.

Although it is a fine little house in a splendid position, Fenton House is better known for its contents than its architecture. The main displays are of china and musical instruments. The china collection contains Staffordshire ware and oriental blue and white as well as one of the finest private collections of 18thC English and continental porcelain in Britain. It was given, along with the house and most of its other contents – furniture, pictures etc – to the National Trust in 1952 by Lady Binning, who lived here from 1936 to 1952. The collection of keyboard instruments includes harpsichords, spinets and virginals dating mainly from the 17thC and 18thC though there are one or two earlier and later models. These instruments were acquired between the wars by Major George Benton Fletcher and given to the Trust in 1937.

Most of the instruments are displayed on the attic floor. In the dining room on the ground floor, the largest room in the house, is a (loan) collection of a dozen or so early paintings by Sir William Nicholson. The rest of the house's contents cover a range of styles and periods and reflect the catholic taste of the wealthy 19thC connoisseur George Salting, from whom Lady Binning inherited them.

> **Fenton House**
> *Open Mar 14.00-18.00 Sat & Sun; Apr-Oct 11.00-18.00 Sat-Wed.*
> Admission charge.
> Guidebook.
> ♿ Access to ground floor only.
> ⊖ Hampstead

### Freud Museum

20 Maresfield Gardens, Hampstead NW3. 071-435 2002.

Hounded by the Nazis, 82-year-old Sigmund Freud fled Vienna in 1938 and came to roost at this house in Hampstead. With him came many of his possessions, including his desk, his famous consulting couch, a large portion of his library and his huge collection of Egyptian, Roman, Greek and Oriental antiquities. All were patiently reassembled by his son Ernst to provide a working environment which resembled as closely as possible the one his father had known and loved in Vienna for the previous 50 years. Tragically Freud only lived a year to enjoy it, but his daughter Anna, a psychoanalytic pioneer in her own right, stayed on in the house continuing the work her father had begun. She died in 1982. In accordance with her wishes the house opened as the Freud Museum four years later. There is an Anna Freud room on the first floor, along with video and exhibition rooms. Downstairs you can see Freud's study and library, preserved by his daughter exactly as they were during his lifetime.

---

**Freud Museum**
*Open 12.00-17.00 Wed-Sun.* Admission charge.
Guided tours. Films. Research facilities.
*Educational facilities:* Tours for schools, lectures.
&#9855; Partial access
&#9758; Finchley Road

---

*Sigmund Freud's analysis couch, Freud Museum*

## Fulham Palace

Fulham Palace, Bishop's Avenue, Fulham SW6. 071-736 3233.
Surrounded by lawn and a walled kitchen garden, Fulham
Palace is set within Bishop's Park, close to the Thames. A
red-brick Tudor Manor House, but on a site that dates back
to the 11thC, this was, until the 1970s, the official residence
of the Bishop of London. Now the local authority runs it and
provides monthly guided tours of the grounds, chapel and
unfurnished Great Hall and drawing room. Two further
rooms on the ground floor are earmarked for a small
museum covering the history of the palace and the various
bishops who have lived there. The museum is due to open in
1992.

---

**Fulham Palace**
Museum *open 14.00-17.00 Wed-Sun (phone to check)*. Free guided
tours *second Sun of each month, starting at 14.00 in the palace
courtyard*. Admission charge.
&#9855; Full access. Toilet.
&#9737; Putney Bridge

---

## Ham House

Ham, Richmond, Surrey. 081-940 1950.
A country house on the banks of the Thames in west London
built by Sir Thomas Vavasour in 1610. Much altered in the
1630s by the Earl of Dysart, today's house is largely the
creation of Dysart's daughter, Elizabeth, and her second
husband, the Duke of Lauderdale. They not only enlarged the
house in the 1670s by adding a new suite of rooms along the
south front on each floor, but also furnished it to a degree of
sumptuousness and luxury remarkable even in that age of
aristocratic opulence. In some rooms the fire tongs and other
chimney furniture are solid silver.

Apart from the decay of some delicate fabrics such as
wall-coverings, curtains and chair covers (replaced where
necessary with reproductions), little has been altered or taken
away since the days of the Lauderdales. As a result Ham
House is the most complete and unchanged 17thC stately
home in the country. It was given to the National Trust by the
Dysart family in 1948.

On show are about 30 rooms on the ground and first floors.
These are mostly the fine rooms where the family lived, and
include the Great Hall, chapel and Long Gallery, as well as
dining, sitting and bedrooms and cosy little closets.
Throughout there are polished wood floors; painted ceilings –

some by the master, Verrio; rich wall coverings in damask, tapestry and gilded leather; fine wood carving and moulding (sold by the foot by the original carpenters); carved and gilded furniture; and a mass of paintings, mostly copies of old masters or family portraits. The Duke and Duchess can be seen together in a fine joint portrait by Sir Peter Lely in the Round Gallery above the Great Hall.

In the first-floor Museum Room above the chapel there is a collection of rare textiles, and next door in the Miniature Room, an important collection of miniatures, including a Hilliard portrait of Queen Elizabeth I. Perhaps the single most impressive feature of the house is the Grand Staircase, a triumphant achievement of bold woodcarving and gilding.

At the end of the tour of the main rooms, you can see some of the servants' rooms and exhibitions on the history of the house and the gardens (also original 17thC). The Back Parlour, the upper servants' sitting room, is panelled very plainly, a relief after the dazzling richness of the main rooms. The restored basement kitchen has a magnificent scrubbed table which is more like a huge chopping block than anything else.

---

**Ham House**

*Open Apr-Sep 11.00-17.30 Tue-Sun. NB: Closed until 1993 for essential structural repairs.* Admission charge.

Guided tours. Guidebook.

*Refreshments:* Afternoon tea served in the tea pavilion *12.00-17.30.*

*Educational facilities:* Tours for schools.

&#x267F; Partial access. Toilet.

&#x2296; Richmond

---

## Hampton Court Palace

East Molesey, Surrey. 081-977 8441.

A forest of red-brick Tudor chimneys marks out this royal riverside palace to the west of London. Essentially, it is split into two main sections, reflecting the two most significant eras in its history. First is the original Tudor palace begun by Cardinal Wolsey in 1514 and then greatly enlarged by King Henry VIII after Wolsey gave Hampton Court to him in a rather one-sided bargain in 1525. Most of the living quarters dating from this time were destroyed in later rebuilding by Wren, but you can still see what are thought to have been Wolsey's rooms with their panelled walls and brightly-coloured ceilings, the magnificent Great Hall with its hammerbeam roof and the richly painted and carved Chapel. Below stairs are the fascinating and well-preserved cellars, butteries and kitchens with cavernous fireplaces where mountains of food were prepared for royal banquets.

The second part consists of the twin sets of magnificent state and private apartments built by Sir Christopher Wren for William III and Queen Mary in the 1690s. Supervised first by Wren and then by Sir John Vanbrugh, many leading artists and craftsmen worked here, including the painters Antonio Verrio, William Kent and Sir James Thornhill, the carver Grinling Gibbons, and the ironworker Jean Tijou. Between them they created suites of splendid rooms, the grander ones entirely covered in flamboyant *trompe-l'oeil* and allegorical paintings, and all beautifully furnished with fine pictures, tapestries and furniture from the royal collection. Worthy of special mention are the lifesize *Yeomen of the Guard* in carved stone and the famous Kneller portraits known as the *Hampton Court Beauties* in the Queen's Guard Chamber, and the superb patterned array of more than 3000 arms in the King's Guard Chamber. Unfortunately, most of the other King's State Apartments have been closed since 1986 because of a serious fire, but they are expected to reopen in 1992. It is worth noting, incidentally, how both the king's and queen's State Apartments start with a Guard Chamber for protection, and then become progressively less public, ending up with a private bedroom.

The finest pictures in the palace are grouped together in the Renaissance Picture Gallery. Here you will see many old masters, including works by Cranach and Steenwyck, Correggio and Titian. You should also make sure you go to the Mantegna Gallery, reached from the Pond Garden between the palace and the river, to see Andrea Mantegna's nine-canvas series of *The Triumph of Caesar*, one of the greatest works of the Renaissance. Nearby are the Great Vine, still producing grapes 200 years after it was planted, the detached Banqueting House overlooking the river, the Tudor real tennis court (still used by a local club) and, of course, the famous 17thC maze, a labyrinth of hedges in which it is only too easy to get hopelessly lost!

The **Embroiderers' Guild** (Apartment 41 in the palace) has a fine collection of historic embroidery, items from which are sometimes on display in its exhibition room. For information, phone: 081-943 1229 between *10.30-16.00 Mon-Fri*.

**Hampton Court Palace**
*Open mid Mar-mid Oct 10.15-18.00 Mon, 09.30-18.00 Tue-Sun; mid Oct-mid Mar 10.15-16.30 Mon, 09.30-16.30 Tue-Sun.* Tennis Court and Banqueting House *closed in winter.* Admission charge. Shop. Guided tours. Guidebook. Films. Research facilities.
*Refreshments*: Licensed restaurant serving hot meals *Mar-Oct 11.00-14.15.* Café serving drinks, sandwiches and cakes *10.00-16.00 ( to 17.30 Mar-Oct).*
*Educational facilities*: Tours for schools, worksheets, lectures.
🔈 Full access arranged if 24 hours notice of visit is given.
≩ Hampton Court

## Hogarth's House

Hogarth Lane, Great West Road, Chiswick W4. 081-994 6757. Hard though it is to believe as the Great West Road thunders by beyond the garden wall, this delightful little house was used by the 18thC artist William Hogarth as his country retreat from 1749 until his death in 1764. An independent, truculent character, Hogarth was one of the finest painters of

*Hogarth's House*

his time and noted for his satirical comments on contemporary life. His work reached a particularly wide audience because of the cheaply priced engravings he made of his paintings.

Rescued from destruction early this century, the house was opened to the public as a gallery in 1902. The five small, panelled rooms do not, unfortunately, contain any of his paintings, but there is a large collection of his engravings, including his most famous narratives, *The Rake's Progress, An Election Entertainment, The Harlot's Progress, Marriage à la Mode,* and *Industry and Idleness.* The original paintings for the first two of these are in Sir John Soane's Museum (see page 132).

---

**Hogarth's House**

*Open Apr-Sep 11.00-18.00 Mon & Wed-Sat, 14.00-18.00 Sun; Oct-Mar 11.00-16.00 Mon & Wed-Sat, 14.00-16.00 Sun. Closed first two weeks in Sep.* Admission free.

Guided tours. Guidebook. Research facilities.

&#9855; Access to ground floor only.

&#10050; Turnham Green

---

## Keats House

Keats Grove, Hampstead NW3. 071-435 2062.

The romantic poet John Keats lived in this small but elegant Regency house from 1819 until his early death (in Rome) in 1821. Whilst here he wrote some of his best work, including *Ode to a Nightingale*, composed under a plum tree (now replaced) in the garden on a single morning. In his day, the

*Keats House*

house formed two separate dwellings. He shared the left-hand-side of the house (as you face it) with a bachelor friend Charles Brown. The girl he fell in love with but did not live to marry, Fanny Brawne, occupied the right-hand-side with her widowed mother and sisters. Inside you can see Keats' sitting room and bedroom, the former practically unchanged, as well as the rooms used by Brown and Mrs Brawne and her girls, including the basement kitchens and cellars. Relics of the poet and his family and friends are also on show. The Keats Memorial Library is next door.

---

**Keats House**

*Open Apr-Oct 14.00-18.00 Mon-Fri, 10.00-13.00 & 14.00-17.00 Sat, 14.00-17.00 Sun; Nov-Mar 13.00-17.00 Mon-Fri, 10.00-13.00 & 14.00-17.00 Sat, 14.00-17.00 Sun.* Admission free.
Guided tours. Guidebook. Films. Research facilities.
♿ No access
⊖ Hampstead

---

## Kensington Palace

Kensington Palace W8. 071-937 9561.
Much of Kensington Palace provides living accommodation for the Prince and Princess of Wales, other members of the royal family, and grace and favour tenants, but since 1899 the most magnificent rooms – the first-floor state apartments facing Kensington Gardens – have been open to the public. These, with their Grinling Gibbons carvings, rich decoration and fine furniture and paintings, were originally built by Sir Christopher Wren in the 1690s for William III and Queen Mary. The king and queen each had a separate suite, complete with long gallery and separate staircase, and these are what visitors see today, along with some magnificent state rooms.

The Queen's apartments – gallery, dining room, drawing room and bedchamber – are mostly panelled and contain much original furniture and numerous royal portraits and other pictures by artists such as Kneller, Lely, Dahl, Van Dyck, Teniers and Bassano. Kneller's imperial portrait of Peter the Great in armour, painted during the Czar's visit to London in 1698, is the most impressive.

The four lofty state rooms, designed by Colen Campbell for George I in about 1720, are decorated with glorious painted ceilings, gilding and other rich effects by William Kent. High and square, the Cupola Room was the principal state room of the palace and was intended by Kent to conjure up an image of Roman grandeur for the new Hanoverian dynasty. Another

*Kensington Palace*

state room, the Council Chamber, was redecorated later, in Regency style, and now contains an interesting group of pictures and objects relating to the 1851 Great Exhibition and other 19thC extravaganzas.

In the king's apartments the highlight must be the amazing Grand Staircase with its walls and ceiling covered in paintings on stretched canvas by Kent. These are his greatest achievement as a decorative painter. The figures crowding the upper part are mostly identifiable portraits and include the artist himself with his mistress and two pupils on the north side. The king's 96ft (30m) gallery and drawing room are filled with paintings, some of them good ones by Rubens, Snyders and Van Dyck, others by lesser artists and not so good.

Three of the king's apartments were converted a century after his time for use by the Duchess of Kent and her daughter, later Queen Victoria. Recently restored, all now contain pictures, sculpture, furniture and other things owned by, or connected with, Queen Victoria and Prince Albert. There are busts by Mary Thorneycroft and pictures by Watts, Beechey and Maclise. In the bedroom, near Hayter's large painting of Victoria and Albert's marriage is the cot used by all Victoria's children. The bed was not used by Victoria.

The rooms beneath the State Apartments, in one of which Queen Victoria was born, are the setting for a dazzling array of court dress for men and women. But although the splendid costumes date back as far as 1750, the main attraction for many people will be one of the most modern additions to the collection: the wedding dress of the current Princess of Wales.

---

**Kensington Palace**
*Open 09.00-17.00 Mon-Sat, 11.00-17.00 Sun.* Admission charge.
Guided tours. Guidebook.
*Educational facilities*: Tours for schools, worksheets.
🚻 Partial access
⊖ Queensway, High Street Kensington, Notting Hill

---

### Kenwood House and The Iveagh Bequest
Hampstead Lane, Hampstead NW3. 081-348 1286.
Kenwood is a great cream stuccoed mansion set in its own grounds in the northern part of Hampstead Heath. Originally built about 1700, Robert Adam transformed it in the 1760s and 70s into a great neo-classical villa for the Earl of Mansfield, complete with suites of custom-built furniture. Emptied of its contents when the Mansfields sold up after the First World War, the house was rescued from suburban development by the Earl of Iveagh, head of the Guinness brewing family, who bought it to house his art collection in 1925. When he died two years later, both house and collection were bequeathed to the nation and opened to the public in 1928.

The Iveagh Bequest is a fairly small collection of about 70 paintings, but because of its quality and popularity, is well-known all over the world. Of its three main sections, the largest is made up of English portraits from the second half of the 18thC. Reynolds, Gainsborough and Romney account for nearly 30 pictures between them; Gainsborough's portrait of *Mary, Countess Howe* being the best-known, and probably the most famous image in the whole collection. The old master section consists mainly of 17thC Dutch and Flemish works, with portraits and figure subjects by Bol, Snyders, Van Dyck, Vermeer and Rembrandt, and landscapes and marine paintings by Ostade, Cuyp, the Van de Veldes and Wynants. The highlights are a Rembrandt *Self-Portrait* and Vermeer's *The Guitar Player*, the only Vermeer on show in Britain outside the National Gallery and the Royal Collection. The smallest group of pictures represents French rococo art and includes works by Pater and Boucher.

Apart from the Iveagh Bequest, the main attraction of Kenwood is the Adam interiors, particularly the blue and gold barrel-ceilinged library, which some experts think is Adam's finest creation. Slowly Adam furniture is being reintroduced into the house following the dispersals of the 1920s. Some of it consists of rediscovered pieces originally commissioned for Kenwood.

Other things to see are the exhibition on the history of the house in Lady Mansfield's Dressing Room on the ground floor, and collections of 18thC and 19thC jewellery, Georgian shoe buckles and portrait miniatures in the bedchambers on the first floor.

---

**Kenwood House** and **The Iveagh Bequest**
*Open Good Fri or 1 Apr (whichever is earlier)-30 Sep 10.00-18.00 Mon-Sun; 1 Oct to Maundy Thur or 31 March (whichever is earlier) 10.00-16.00 Mon-Sun.* Admission free.
Shop. Guided tours. Guidebook.
*Refreshments*: Licensed café/restaurant serving full meals, light lunches and snacks *12.00-17.30 Mon-Sun (to 15.30 in winter)*. The Old Kitchen Restaurant serves traditional Sunday lunch *11.00-15.00 Sun.*
&#9855; Full access. Toilet.
&#9758; Golders Green (then bus 210)

---

### Kew Palace

Royal Botanic Gardens, Kew, Richmond, Surrey.
081-940 3321
Built in the 17thC as the country retreat for a City merchant, this pretty brick house in Kew Gardens became a royal palace, albeit a small one, in the early 18thC when the royal family adopted Kew as a summer resort for the court. The last royal residents were George III and Queen Charlotte, who used it as a temporary summer residence when construction of a new palace nearby began. Later the building work was abandoned and the king retired to Windsor with mental problems. But the Queen continued to use the house as a private retreat right until her death in 1818. She and King George were the only reigning monarchs who actually lived here.

On show today are the king's rooms – dining room, breakfast room and bedchamber – and the queen's rooms – boudoir, drawing room and bedchamber – plus various ante-rooms and closets, the library and the pages' waiting room. All have been restored with decorations and furnishings of the early 19thC, the period of royal occupation. Besides some nice furniture and a handful of royal portraits by Gainsborough, Zoffany and Benjamin West, you will see personal relics of George III and his family, including the king's walking stick, his son's fishing tackle, and children's playthings.

Also in Kew Gardens is **Queen Charlotte's Cottage**, a summer house built in 1770 and used by Queen Charlotte and her family for teas, suppers and picnics. *Open Apr-Sep 11.00-17.30 Sat-Sun & Bank Hols.* Admission charge.

See also the Marianne North Gallery in Art Galleries (page 143), and Kew Gardens Gallery in Exhibition Spaces (page 164).

---

**Kew Palace**
*Open Apr-Sep 11.00-17.30 Mon-Sun.* Admission charge.
Shop. Guided tours. Guidebook. Research facilities.
*Educational facilities*: Tours for schools.
& Partial access
⊖ Kew Gardens

---

## Leighton House

12 Holland Park Road W14. 071-602 3316.                    3 A6

Leighton House, one of the finest examples of the 'Aesthetic' style of interior decoration in England, belonged to Frederick, Lord Leighton (1830-96), the great Victorian classical painter and President of the Royal Academy. Leighton started building the house in 1866, his intention being to create not just a home and studio but a structure in which every element – design, decoration and furnishing – harmonised to express his own high ideals of beauty. Collaborating with architect George Aitchison and fellow artists like William de Morgan, Edgar Boehm and Randolph Caldecott, he set about creating a suite of richly-coloured rooms with ebonised and gilded woodwork, which were then filled with pictures, ceramics and objets d'art brought from all over the world. The whole process never stopped during the 30 years Leighton occupied the house.

Sadly, all the furnishings and works of art in the house had to be sold on Leighton's death to fund one of his character-istically generous bequests. But some paintings and drawings were bought back to launch the museum created to preserve the remarkable house. Over the years this small nucleus has grown into a notable collection of High Victorian aesthetic art, with important works by Leighton himself and other artists such as Burne-Jones, Millais, Alma-Tadema and G. F. Watts. Some of the pictures on show are on loan from other collections. Together, the collections and the faithfully restored interiors of the house evoke the late 19thC high society artistic world in which Leighton – the only artist ever made a peer – lived.

As you tour the house you will see various rooms – the library, drawing room, dining room, Silk Room (so-called because of its green silk wall coverings) and studio. But the highlight is the Arab Hall, based on a banqueting room in a Moorish palace in Palermo. Added on to the house in the 1870s, the hall was built as a showcase for the superb Islamic tiles of the 16thC and 17thC which Leighton collected on his youthful travels in the Middle East. The Hall also has a gilt mosaic frieze by Walter Crane, and is overlooked by an original zenana (fretted balcony) brought from Cairo.

---

**Leighton House**
*Open 11.00-17.30 Mon-Sat.* Admission free.
Shop. Guided tours. Guidebook.
*Educational facilities:* Lectures.
&#x267F; Partial access
&#x2296; High Street Kensington (then bus 9, 10, 27, 28, 31, 33, 49)

---

## Linley Sambourne House

18 Stafford Terrace W8. 081-994 1019.                              3 B5

This large terraced house off Kensington High Street is one of the wonders of London for anybody interested in domestic interiors. For nearly a century from the 1870s to the 1970s it was the home of the Linley Sambourne family and their descendants. *Punch* cartoonist Edward Linley Sambourne was the first occupant. Apart from being a gifted artist, he was also a compulsive shopper. During the 40 years he lived in the house he gradually filled its five storeys with pictures, furniture and a mass of other objects decorative and useful. At the same time he covered every available surface – wall, floors, ceilings, even some of the windows – in the rich but sombre colours so popular at the time. Morris wallpaper is much in evidence. Fortunately his descendants made few changes after his death in 1910, so what we have today is a unique survival of a Victorian house furnished by an artist completely immersed in the taste of the time. It is also a fine memorial to its jovial and talented creator. Many of the pictures and drawings that thickly plaster the walls are by him or members of his wide circle of artist friends, and there are many photographs too as a reminder that Linley Sambourne was very interested in this emerging art. On show are the ground floor dining room, morning room and WC, first-floor drawing room, second floor bedrooms and bathroom, and top floor studio where Linley Sambourne worked. As an indication of its aesthetic value, the house is run by the country's leading Victorian amenity group, the Victorian Society.

---

**Linley Samborne House**
*Open 1 Mar-31 Oct 10.00-16.00 Wed, 14.00-17.00 Sun.* Admission charge.
Shop. Guided tours. Guidebook.
&#x267f; No access
&#x2296; High Street Kensington

---

## Little Holland House
40 Beeches Avenue, Carshalton, Surrey. 081-773 4555.
An Arts and Crafts house created by artist, designer and craftsman Frank Dickinson (1874-1961). Inspired by the ideas of John Ruskin and William Morris, Dickinson designed and built the house himself, and then went on to make the contents with his own hands. On show are paintings, furniture, copperwork and other craft objects, all Dickinson's work. Notable features of the house include the master bedroom with its painted frieze, the carved timbers in the living room, and the decorated fireplace surrounds.

---

**Little Holland House**
*Open Mar-Oct 13.00-18.00 1st Sun of each month plus Bank Hols and preceding Sun.* Admission free.
Shop. Guided tours. Guidebook.
&#x267f; Partial – ground floor only.
&#x279c; Carshalton Beeches

---

## Marble Hill House
Richmond Road, Twickenham, Middlesex. 081-892 5115.
This beautiful Palladian villa on the banks of the Thames in west London was built in the 1720s as a summer retreat for Henrietta Howard, mistress to George II, and later Countess of Suffolk. Colen Campbell designed the house and Charles Bridgeman, the royal gardener, landscaped the grounds around it, with assistance from Henrietta's friend and neighbour, the poet Alexander Pope.

Bought for the nation from the Cunard family in 1902, the

house lay stripped and empty for many years before being opened as a historic house museum in 1966. Now painted a brilliant white and standing out starkly from the surrounding greenery, it is home to an important and growing collection of paintings and furniture dating from the early 18thC. Some things, like the views of Rome by Panini, were originally commissioned for the house and have now been restored to their rightful home after long absences.

Visitors see three storeys of the house, each containing about five rooms. The main ones are the richly decorated, double-height Great Room on the first floor, and the recently-restored gallery on the second. A superb mahogany staircase leads up to the first floor. The pictures, including portraits of Lady Suffolk and her circle, are by artists such as Hogarth, Kneller, Reynolds, Hayman and Wilson. Museum policy is to move pictures and furniture around frequently as new acquisitions are being made all the time.

---

**Marble Hill House**
*Open Good Fri or 1 Apr (whichever is earlier)-30 Sep 10.00-18.00 Mon-Sun; 1 Oct-Maundy Thur or 31 Mar (whichever is earlier) 10.00-16.00 Mon-Sun.* Admission free.
Shop. Guided tours. Guidebook.
*Refreshments*: Restaurant serving hot & cold light meals *Apr-Sep 10.00-18.00 Mon-Sun.*
*Educational facilities*: Tours for schools, lectures.
⟨&⟩ Partial access – ground floor only.
⊖ Richmond

---

## Old Battersea House

Vicarage Crescent, Battersea SW11. 071-788 1341.
Built in the 17thC and said to have been designed by Sir Christopher Wren, Old Battersea House is both a private home and the setting for part of the De Morgan Foundation collection of Pre-Raphaelite art. There are ceramics by William de Morgan himself, and paintings and drawings by Evelyn de Morgan, her uncle Roddam Spencer Stanhope, J. M. Strudwick and Cadogan Cowper. All the works are on the ground floor. A visit to nearby Old Battersea Church is usually included in the guided tour.

---

**Old Battersea House**
*Open by appointment – usually Wed afternoon. Write in advance to De Morgan Foundation, 21 St Margaret's Crescent, Putney, London SW15 6HL.* Admission charge.
⟨&⟩ Full access, except for awkward entrance steps.
Bus  239

**Osterley Park House**

Isleworth, Middlesex. 081-560 3918.

A large country house set in 140 acres (57ha) of landscaped park in west London. Built originally in Elizabethan times for the prince of London merchants, Sir Thomas Gresham, it was transformed into a neo-classical villa in the 18thC by the Childs, a wealthy banking family. Francis Child and his brother Robert employed the leading architects of their day, Sir William Chambers and Robert Adam, to create a splendid Pantheon of the Arts and Sciences, with every little feature a reference to some aspect of the literature or architecture of ancient Greece and Rome. The classical allusions may be lost on us today, but we can still appreciate, or rather wonder at, the truly gorgeous and impressive interior decoration of the house – the plasterwork, the colours, the painted ceilings, the damask and silk-lined walls. Although there are many other things to see in the house – Gobelin tapestries, an eight-poster bed conceived as a Temple of Venus, Chinese and Japanese cabinets and specially-made furniture painted to fit in with the overall design schemes for certain rooms – Adam's neo-classical interiors are far and away the finest feature of the house.

Entering through the unusual transparent portico on the east front you see the hall, library, 130ft (40m)-long gallery, reception rooms and state bedchamber suite. The colours used range from cool and simple greys, blues, greens and yellows to blazing red and gold. Upstairs, at the top of the Grand Staircase are two bedrooms and two dressing rooms, much less grand, but still a feast for the eyes. Perhaps the most unusual room in the house – in terms of decoration at least – is the ground-floor Etruscan dressing room, with its walls covered in dancing maidens and curly arabesques. Now in the safekeeping of the National Trust, this house really is one of the great English treasures of the 18thC.

---

**Osterley Park House**

*Open Mar 11.00-17.00 Sat & Sun; Apr-Oct 13.00-17.00 Wed-Fri, 11.00-17.00 Sat, Sun & Bank Hols.* Admission charge.

Shop. Guided tours. Guidebook. Research facilities.

*Refreshments*: The Stables tearoom, serving light lunches and teas 11.00-17.00 Tue-Sun.

*Educational facilities*: Tours for schools, worksheets, lectures.

♿ Full access, but difficult entrance steps. Toilet.

⊖ Osterley

## Pitshanger Manor Museum

Mattock Lane, Ealing W5. 081-567 1227.

Originally a 17thC house, Pitshanger Manor was extensively altered and added to in the 1760s, then completely transformed into a beautiful Regency villa between 1800 and 1810 by its then owner, the famous architect Sir John Soane. Ealing Borough now owns it and is slowly restoring it to its former glory after years of decay. As yet the house is sparsely furnished. This just makes it much easier to enjoy the cool light spaces and the splendid interior decoration. Especially remarkable are Soane's richly painted library and breakfast room – a true feast, but for the eyes – and the beautiful plasterwork ceilings in the 1760s eating and drawing rooms. In a later Victorian room off to one side of the house there is a display of Martinware pottery made by the four Martin brothers between 1877 and 1923 at their nearby Southall pottery.

---

**Pitshanger Manor**
*Open 10.00-17.00 Tue-Sat.* Admission free.
Shop. Guided tours. Guidebook.
*Refreshments:* Vending machines dispensing hot & cold drinks.
*Educational facilities:* Tours for schools, workshops.
&#9855; Partial access – ground floor only.
&#9897; Ealing Broadway

---

## Ranger's House

Chesterfield Walk, Blackheath, Greenwich SE10.
081-853 0035.

A modest brick mansion on the edge of Greenwich Park built for a naval officer about 1700, and from 1815 the official residence of the Ranger of the Park. In the middle of the 18thC it was the home of the Earl of Chesterfield, author of the famous *Letters*. Today the house contains portraits and other paintings from the family of the Earls of Suffolk, the Dolmetsch collection of musical instruments, and various pieces of contemporary furniture recently acquired for the house.

The grandest room is the ground floor gallery. Here you can see the pick of the Suffolk Collection – superb full-length family portraits of Jacobean aristocrats in gorgeous costume rendered in immaculate detail. Some are by Cornelius Johnson and Daniel Mytens, but the majority are the work of the little-known and underestimated William Larkin. Other rooms on the ground floor contain pre-Jacobean and 18thC Suffolk portraits, a handful of old masters and, in the Green Silk Parlour, royal portraits, including a voluptuous *Mary of Modena* by Lely.

Upstairs you see the main bedroom of the house furnished in the early Georgian style, plus other rooms containing the 17thC and 18thC string, woodwind and brass instruments collected by Arnold Dolmetsch (1858-1940). The collection has no formal links with the house, being placed here by the GLC as there was plenty of space, but it is nevertheless fascinating and an interesting addition. A pioneer of early music studies, some of the instruments were actually made by Dolmetsch himself, and musical prints and portraits add a human dimension to the collection.

> **Ranger's House**
> *Open Good Fri or 1 Apr (whichever is earlier)-30 Sep 10.00-18.00 Mon-Sun; 1 Oct-Maundy Thur or 31 Mar (whichever is earlier) 10.00-16.00 Mon-Sun.* Admission free.
> Shop. Guided tours.
> *Educational facilities*: Tours for schools, schoolroom for teaching.
> & Partial access – ground floor only.
> Bus 53

## Sherlock Holmes Museum

221b Baker Street NW1. 071-935 8866.                    1 B5

Here at 221b Baker Street, said to be the actual house on which Conan-Doyle modelled his imaginary 221b, the International Sherlock Holmes Society has recreated the great detective's domestic world, based on detailed study of the stories and using only original Victorian furnishings. Holmes' cluttered sitting room and bedroom are on the first floor. Mrs Bridges' and Dr Watson's rooms are on the floor above. Holmes aficionados will be delighted to see the slipper where Holmes kept his tobacco, his violin and chemistry set, the VR initials on the wall made during target practice, and numerous other little personal touches redolent of the man and his cases. In Watson's room you can sit by the fire and read the stories and period magazines. Almost more fun is browsing through the amazing messages addressed to Holmes at this address, including offers of marriage. Every one gets a personal reply.

> **Sherlock Holmes Museum**
> *Open 10.00-18.00 Mon-Sun.* Admission charge.
> Shop. Guided tours. Guidebook.
> *Refreshments*: Licensed restaurant serving traditional English food 11.00-15.00 & 18.00-23.00 Mon-Fri.
> *Educational facilities:* Tours for schools, lectures.
> & No access
> ⊖ Baker Street

## Sir John Soane's Museum

13 Lincoln's Inn Fields WC2. 071-405 2107.                    5 A2

This extraordinary house-cum-museum is one of the sights of London. Every part of it reflects the architectural ingenuity and love of beauty of its creator, Sir John Soane, one of the leading architects of Regency England. Having designed the house himself, he spent over 20 years embellishing the interior, before leaving it to the nation as a public museum on his death in 1837. It has been little changed since.

At the front you have the main reception rooms, alive with colour from the decoratively-painted surfaces, furnishings and works of art. At the back is what might be called the museum part of the house. Here in a warren of unusual rooms with strange names like the Monk's Parlour and the Sepulchral Chamber, you will see some of Soane's cleverest solutions to the problems of letting in light or creating space; the hinged frames in the picture gallery are a case in point. Here also you will see some of the greatest treasures in the house, including the sarcophagus of Seti I, excavated from the Valley of the Kings in Egypt in 1817, and architectural drawings by Piranesi and Clérisseau, the masters of this popular 18thC genre.

In the tradition of the times, Soane was an admirer of classical culture, so the house is filled with Greek vases, Roman urns, busts and reliefs and other antiquities. But all Soane's furniture – mostly contemporary – is also still in the house, as is his picture collection, mainly English paintings of the 18thC and early 19thC. As well as works by Lawrence, Reynolds, Canaletto and Turner, it includes William Hogarth's original paintings for two of his most famous series of prints, *The Rake's Progress* and *An Election Entertainment*.

---

**Sir John Soane's Museum**
*Open 10.00-17.00 Tue-Sat (also 18.00-21.00 first Tue of each month).* Admission free.
Shop. Guided tours. Guidebook. Research facilities.
*Educational facilities*: Tours for schools.
&#x267F; No access
&#x2296; Holborn

---

## Soseki Museum in London

80b The Chase, Clapham SW4. 071-720 8718.

A small museum devoted to the life and work of the Japanese novelist and scholar of English literature, Natsume Soseki

(1867-1916). Soseki spent two unhappy years in England on a government scholarship from 1900 to 1902. As well as a portrait of the writer, the museum contains photographs, books, newspapers and magazines relating mainly to Soseki's life in London; an entire collection of Soseki's writings; critical works on the author; and a selection of books on modern Japanese literature.

Opened in 1984 by Soseki admirer Sammy Tsunematsu, the museum is on the first floor of a terraced house in Clapham, directly opposite the last of the many lodgings Soseki used during his brief London sojourn.

---

**Soseki Museum in London**
*Open Feb-Sep by appointment only, 14.00-17.00 Wed, 10.00-12.00 & 14.00-17.00 Sat, 14.00-17.00 Sun.* Admission charge.
Guided tours. Research facilities.
⟨&⟩ No access
⊖ Clapham North

---

## Spencer House

27 St James's Place SW1. 071-409 0526.                    4 D4

This grand nobleman's town house near St James's Palace was built in the 1760s for the young Earl Spencer and used by the Spencer family (of Princess of Wales fame) until the 1920s. Gutted and converted into utilitarian offices during World War II, it was acquired by Lord Rothschild in the 1980s and restored to something like its former glory, especially the fine rooms along the west front overlooking Green Park, which are the ones the public sees.

These rooms are all richly decorated in the neo-classical style with painted ceilings, carved friezes and gilded mouldings. Dark mahogany doors, crystal chandeliers, large mirrors and gay carpets enhance the atmosphere of cultured luxury. All the furniture, drawn from a variety of sources and some of it now restored to the house for which it was originally made, is contemporaneous and, with only two exceptions, English. The pictures include portraits by Reynolds and Gainsborough and large historical and mythological scenes by Benjamin West, lent by the Queen. The two grandest rooms are the ground-floor dining room and huge first-floor Grand Saloon. The two most interesting rooms from the decorative point of view are the Palm Room – a mass of gilded wooden palm fronds – and the Painted Room – its walls completely covered with brightly-coloured pictures and arabesque designs.

Inevitably there is a lot of modern work in the house, from brand new silk brocade wall hangings to carved marble fireplaces. A good feature of the tour, which takes about an hour, is the way the guides draw your attention to the work of restoration, not excluding the gilded polystyrene mouldings in Lady Spencer's Room which in other places might be rather frowned upon. Another nice touch is the open fire in the entrance hall – very welcoming on a cold winter's day.

---

**Spencer House**
*Open Feb-Jul & Sep-Dec 10.00-17.00 Sun for guided tours. Tours every 15 minutes 10.45-16.45. Phone 071-499 8620 10.00-13.00 Tue-Fri to book a tour in advance.*
Guidebook.
🚻 Full access
⊖ Piccadilly Circus

---

## Syon House
Syon Park, Brentford, Middlesex. 081-560 0881.
This riverside country house in west London stands in a large park with gardens by Capability Brown sweeping down to the Thames. The battlemented exterior conceals a suite of magnificent neo-classical rooms by Robert Adam (1728-92), an architect and interior designer of great genius. From the cool, almost monochrome Great Hall with its classical statues and black and white patterned floor, you move into the ante room, a riot of gilding and colour with a bright scagliola floor, painted ceiling and large gilded figures high up round the entablature. The 60ft (19m) dining room in white and gold with apses at either end is rather more restful and sober, but the Red Drawing Room plunges you back into luxury and opulence. Both the crimson silk wall coverings and the carpet were made in London in the 1760s, the latter especially for this room. Virtually all the pictures here are Stuart portraits by artists like Van Dyck and Sir Peter Lely. The other major Adam room is the 136ft (42m) Long Gallery. Lined with books, doors and fireplaces down one side and windows and mirrors down the other, it was designed in an Elizabethan-Jacobean style rather than the usual neo-classical. As with other rooms, it contains specially made furniture.

The last room visitors see is the 19thC Print Room, actually a bedroom but containing many portraits of people connected with the history of the house, mainly members of the Northumberland family. Originally built as a monastery in the 15thC, Syon was turned into a house by Protector Somerset after the Dissolution of the Monasteries, and then assigned to the Northumberland family by Queen Elizabeth in 1597. It is still one of the family homes of the Dukes of Northumberland.

---

**Syon House**
*Open Easter-Sep 12.00-17.00 Sun-Thur; Oct 12.00-17.00 Sun.*
Admission charge.
Shop. Guided tours. Guidebook.
*Refreshments*: Licensed restaurant serving hot & cold meals
(reserve) *12.00-14.30 Sun-Fri.* Café serving light meals, sandwiches
and cakes. The Bakery, coffee shop, serving cakes and pastries.
Both *open 10.00-17.30 Mon-Sun.*
&#9855; Full access. Toilet.
&#8788; Syon Lane

---

## Wellington Museum

Apsley House, 149 Piccadilly, Hyde Park Corner W1.     4 B5
071-499 5676.

This great London landmark was the town house of Arthur Wellesley, first Duke of Wellington and conqueror of Napoleon. He bought it from his brother in 1817 for £42,000 and used it until his death in 1852, having spent vast sums enlarging and beautifying it. Because of its size and position on what was then the western limit of London, it was nicknamed No. 1 London. The original house had been designed by Robert Adam in the 1770s for Lord Apsley, later second Earl Bathurst. In 1947 the 7th Duke of Wellington gave it to the nation along with its fabulous collection of paintings, porcelain, plate, sculpture, orders and decorations and personal mementoes. Some apartments were retained for the use of the family, but it can't be a very quiet place to sleep!

There are six main rooms on show, all on the first floor overlooking Hyde Park or Hyde Park Corner. For the most part they are gorgeously decorated with silk wall hangings and gilded mouldings. What little furniture there is is generally ranged along the walls. The red ottomans are thoughtfully provided for public use. There are also many busts and statues, particularly in the main entrance hall where they are forested in an unusual and attractive way. The largest piece is the huge nude of Napoleon at the foot of the main staircase. Carved by Antonio Canova for the emperor himself, Napoleon disliked its athleticism and had it packed away in the Louvre. Later the British Government bought it and presented it to Wellington.

The chief feature of the main rooms, and also of the Inner Hall on the ground floor, is the picture collection. There are some 200 paintings altogether, from full-length portraits and large battle scenes to tiny cabinet pictures and altar pieces. Most of them were acquired by the Iron Duke, either through conquest, purchase or gift. Over 80 came to him following his victory in 1813 at Vittoria in Spain. Generally, they are plastered thickly over the walls, especially in the top-lit Waterloo Gallery, by far the largest room in the house. This is apparently how the Duke liked them.

The collection falls into two parts. The first consists of contemporary pictures, including portraits of the Duke and of his comrades-in-arms (especially in the Striped Drawing Room), and many portraits of Napoleon, Josephine and Napoleon's family. There are also two famous paintings of Waterloo; one, in the Inner Hall, showing Highlanders standing firm against a French cavalry charge. In the Dining Room portraits of the allied sovereigns – all presented to Wellington – look down on the long dining table with its fantastic silver centrepiece from Portugal – another gift. The other part of the collection consists of old masters ranging in date from about 1500 to the late 18thC. Correggio, Van Dyck, Elsheimer, Rubens, Goya, Guercino, Brueghel and many other important artists are represented. Among the handful of works by Velázquez is his famous *Waterseller of Seville*.

The other main collection in the house is the Duke's incredible china and plate, including gold and silver. There must be half a dozen dinner services at least, all beautifully painted, decorated or engraved. Perhaps the most extraordinary and historically interesting is the Egyptian Service in the special China and Plate Room. Conspicuous by its outrageous 20ft (6m)-long centrepiece in the form of Egyptian temples, it was given by Napoleon to Josephine as a divorce present!

Last but not least among all this grandeur there are some personal possessions of the Duke's on show, including some of his war trophies. These include the swords of his two greatest adversaries, Napoleon, and Tippoo Sahib, the Indian prince Wellington defeated at Seringapatam in 1797.

---

**Wellington Museum**
*Open 11.00-17.00 Tue-Sun. NB: Closed until the end of 1993 for essential maintenance work.* Admission charge.
Shop. Guided tours. Guidebook.
&#9855; Partial access. Toilet.
&#8854; Hyde Park Corner

**Wesley's House**
47 City Road EC1. 071-253 2262.
In this Georgian terraced house just north of the City, John
Wesley, the founder of Methodism, lived for the last 12 years
of his long life. Born in Lincolnshire in 1703, he came to the
house in 1779 and died in the house in 1791. Little changed
since, and still containing many of his personal effects (as

*Wesley's House*

well as historic Methodist documents), it is now a place of pilgrimage for Methodists from all over the world.

All seven rooms on show are very plain, with bare wooden floors, no curtains, uncoloured walls and plain brown wainscoting, door and window frames. Wesley's own rooms were on the first floor. The main room at the front was his study. It still contains his magnificent walnut bureau and many of his books, plus his reading chair and longcase clock. In the case in the corner you can see Wesley's travelling robe, three-cornered hat, preaching bands and buckled shoes. The bedroom behind, where he died, contains more of his furniture, and Romney's portrait of him at the age of 86. In the tiny closet leading off the bedroom, the spiritual centre of the whole museum, Wesley began each day at 4am praying at the little table and kneeler.

Upstairs on the third floor are the room used by Charles Wesley when visiting his brother John, and the Museum Room. Here you can see a few of Wesley's personal possessions such as his glasses, fork, nightcap and spurs, and the electrical machine with which he treated patients at his clinics. Wesley's tomb is in the churchyard behind the Methodist chapel next door to the house, and the Museum of Methodism (see page 52) is in the undercroft of the chapel.

---

**Wesley's House**
*Open 10.00-16.00 Mon-Sat.* Admission charge.
Guided tours. Guidebook. Research facilities.
*Refreshments*: Coffee bar serving drinks and snacks.
*Educational facilities*: Tours for schools, lectures.
&#x267F; Partial access – ground floor only.
&#x2296; Old Street

---

## William Morris Gallery

Lloyd Park, Forest Road, Walthamstow E17. 081-527 3782.
William Morris senior worked in the City and made enough money to buy this modest 18thC mansion in east London where his family lived from 1848-56. Now in local council ownership, it has, since 1950, housed a fine collection of works illustrating the achievements of William Morris junior, the pioneer designer, writer and socialist who died in 1896.

Morris and his colleagues in Morris & Co worked in many different fields, and the collection's varied contents reflect them all – wallpapers, printed and woven textiles, embroideries, rugs and carpets, furniture, stained glass, ceramics and printed books (the museum has one of the rare

Kelmscott Chaucers). Also on display are similar works by other members of the Arts and Crafts movement: Arthur Mackmurdo's Century Guild; furniture makers Gimson, Barnsley and Voysey; and stained glass designer Christopher Whall. The Brangwyn gift of paintings and drawings by Sir Frank Brangwyn and the Pre-Raphaelites nicely complements the main holdings of decorative and applied arts.

---

**William Morris Gallery**
*Open 10.00-13.00 & 14.00-17.00 Tue-Sat, 10.00-12.00 & 14.00-17.00 first Sun of each month.* Admission free.
Shop. Guided tours. Research facilities.
*Educational facilities*: Tours for schools, worksheets, lectures, workshops.
&#9855; Partial access – ground floor only.
&#8854; Walthamstow Central

---

## William Morris Society

Kelmscott House, 26 Upper Mall, Hammersmith W6.
081-741 3735.
This handsome 18thC riverside house was the London home of William Morris from 1878 until his death in 1896 and was named after his country home in Oxfordshire, Kelmscott Manor. The famous Hammersmith carpets were woven here in the coach house and the Kelmscott Press operated from 1891 in another house nearby.

Today the William Morris Society maintains a small collection of Morris designs and fabrics in the basement of Kelmscott House. Some pieces are on show, together with a printing press and some of the Kelmscott Press books printed on it. The Society also mounts small temporary exhibitions on Morris and his circle.

---

**William Morris Society**
*Open 13.30-17.30 Thur & Sat.* Admission free.
Guidebook. Research facilities.
*Educational facilities*: Tours for schools.
&#9855; No access
&#8854; Ravenscourt Park

---

# *ART COLLECTIONS*

## Bethlem Royal Hospital Museum

Monks Orchard Road, Beckenham, Kent. 081-777 6611.

Attached to the Bethlem psychiatric hospital (the original Bedlam) is a large and unusual collection of pictures connected with mental disorder. Some were painted by artists with mental problems, others were the work of people who only expressed themselves artistically when under the influence of their disorder. There are actually well over 700 pictures in the collection, but the museum is only big enough for about 60 of them to be put on show. These, however, comprise some of the best known, including watercolours by Richard Dadd and some of Louis Wain's *Kaleidoscopic Cats*. Other artists represented in the collection include William Kurelek, Nijinsky and Charles Sims.

---

**Bethlem Royal Hospital Museum**
*Open 09.30-17.30 Mon-Fri (phone first to confirm times).* Admission free.
Guidebooks. Research facilities.
&#9855; Full access
&#10156; Eden Park

---

## Courtauld Institute Galleries

Somerset House, Strand WC2. 071-873 2526.          4 G3

These suitably formal and academic galleries house the picture collection of the Courtauld Institute of Art, the art history department of London University. The Institute was founded in 1931 and named after its main backer, the industrialist Samuel Courtauld. From gifts of pictures by Courtauld and other collectors, the Institute's collection has grown into one of the finest in the world. Spanning 600 years of Western European art, it is especially known for its Impressionist and Post-Impressionist works (galleries 5 and 6). As well as paintings, it also contains prints, drawings, furniture and other objets d'art, including some fine silver made by Courtauld's ancestors in the 18thC (gallery 7).

Once separated, the Institute and its galleries were brought together in this building, the 'Strand block' of Somerset

House, in 1989. The setting is very much in keeping, for the so-called 'Fine Rooms' in which the collection is now displayed were actually purpose-built in the 18thC for various learned societies, including the Royal Academy. The rest of Somerset House was designed for government offices and is still used for that purpose today.

The pictures are hung in 11 galleries on the first and second floors. As funds permit, the rooms are slowly being redecorated in their original 18thC colours. The overall arrangement is broadly chronological, except that the earliest pictures (from Italy and the Netherlands) are in Gallery 11, and Gallery 8 is set aside as an art history educational room. The Prints and Drawings exhibition room is at the main entrance into Somerset House, on the other side of the archway from the main gallery entrance.

*Gallery 1:* 15thC and 16thC Renaissance art: paintings, marriage chests, Italian majolica, plus a Roman altar as a reminder of the classical origins of the Renaissance.

*Gallery 2:* 16thC and 17thC Italian art and Rubens. Pictures by Caravaggio, Lorenzo Lotto and Van Dyck as well as Rubens. Islamic metalwork and Venetian and German glass.

*Gallery 3:* Rubens and 17thC art, including works by Pietro da Cortona and Domenico Fetti. Teniers sketches and other small panel paintings in the display cases.

*Gallery 4:* Giambattista Tiepolo and 18thC Italian art.

*Gallery 5:* Impressionists and Post-Impressionists. Famous works by all the masters, including Manet, Monet, Renoir, Degas, Pissarro, Sisley, Gauguin, Cézanne and Van Gogh.

*Gallery 6:* Post-Impressionists (mainly Cézanne, Seurat and Toulouse-Lautrec) and Modigliani.

*Gallery 7:* Decorative arts and portraits. 18thC British furniture and silver plus paintings by Gainsborough, Allan Ramsay, Romney, Raeburn and Beechey.

*Gallery 8:* Thematic displays in 12 screened-off areas. The 'RA line' running round the room about seven feet off the floor is a relic of the Royal Academy's summer exhibitions, held here from 1780-1836. Pictures to which the hanging committee wanted to give special prominence were hung on or below the line.

*Galleries 9 & 10:* 20thC painting and sculpture, mainly by British artists, such as Sickert, Duncan Grant, Ben Nicholson, Prunella Clough and Frank Dobson.

*Gallery 11:* Italian and Netherlandish paintings from the 14thC-16thC.

> **Courtauld Institute Galleries**
> *Open 10.00-18.00 Mon-Sat, 14.00-18.00 Sun.* Admission charge.
> Bookshop. Guided tours. Guidebook. Films. Research facilities.
> *Refreshments*: Café serving drinks, sandwiches and cakes *10.30-17.30.*
> *Educational facilities*: Tours for schools, worksheets, lectures, workshops.
> ♿ Full access. Toilet.
> ⊖ Charing Cross, Holborn

## Dulwich Picture Gallery

College Road, Dulwich SE21. 081-693 5254.

Despite its suburban setting and modest size, Dulwich Picture Gallery contains a collection of old masters worthy of any national gallery. Indeed, most of the pictures were collected in the late 18thC for a projected national gallery for Poland, but in the end it never materialised because of the unexpected dismemberment of the country in 1795. The stateless collection was then inherited by painter Sir Francis Bourgeois who left it, along with his own pictures, to Dulwich College, mainly because the College undertook to allow the public in to see it. Hung in a special gallery designed by Sir John Soane, the collection was opened to the public in 1817, beating the National Gallery by seven years to the title of first public art gallery in Britain.

There are 12 small, top-lit galleries altogether and about half the gallery's 650 paintings are on show at any one time. The collection is particularly strong in 17thC and 18thC painting, mainly Dutch, Flemish, French and English, but there are also some Spanish and Italian works. All the big names are represented: Claude, Poussin, Rembrandt, Rubens, Van Dyck, Gainsborough, Reynolds, Velázquez, Murillo, Canaletto and Tiepolo. Amongst the famous pictures on show, look out for Murillo's *Flower Girl* (Room 3), Poussin's *Triumph of David* (Room 4), Gerrit Dou's *Lady Playing the Clavichord* (Room 11) and the Claude Lorrain landscapes in Room 12. Rooms 1 and 9 contain marvellous 18thC English portraits. Rooms 7 and 8 are often used for changing exhibitions, loan or collection-based.

Distributed around the gallery are some fine pieces of 18thC furniture bequeathed by Mrs Desenfans, wife of the man originally commissioned by the King of Poland to buy pictures for his country. The entrance hall contains displays about the history of the gallery, together with portraits of the founders and donors. Mr and Mrs Desenfans and Sir Francis Bourgeois lie in the amber-lit mausoleum which Soane designed as part of the gallery.

> **Dulwich Picture Gallery**
> *Open 10.00-13.00 & 14.00-17.00 Tue-Fri, 11.00-17.00 Sat, 14.00-17.00 Sun.* Admission charge.
> Shop. Guided tours. Guidebook. Films.
> *Educational facilities:* Tours for schools, worksheets, lectures, workshops.
> &#x267f; Full access. Toilet.
> &#x2720; North Dulwich, West Dulwich

## Heinz Gallery

21 Portman Square W1. 071-580 5533.      4 B2

Made possible by the generosity of Mr and Mrs Henry Heinz II, this small modern gallery was opened in 1972 in an Adam house just off Portman Square. It is part of the Royal Institute of British Architects (see page 168) and provides an exhibition space for the Drawings Collection of the Institute's British Architectural Library. The largest of its kind in the world, the collection contains over 400,000 drawings, ranging in date from the 15thC to the present day, and illustrating the work of famous architects from Andrea Palladio to Norman Foster.

> **Heinz Gallery**
> *Open during exhibitions 11.00-17.00 Mon-Fri, 10.00-13.00 Sat.* Admission free.
> &#x267f; Full access. Toilet.
> &#x2296; Marble Arch

## Marianne North Gallery

Royal Botanic Gardens, Kew, Richmond, Surrey.
081-940 1171.

The walls of this small Victorian art gallery are literally covered with over 800 brightly coloured oil paintings of plants, landscapes, birds, animals and insects from all over the world. The pictures were given to Kew by their artist, Marianne North, an intrepid Victorian lady who spent 13 years travelling and painting in the 1870s and 80s. Miss North also paid for this special gallery in which to display them. It was opened in 1882.

> **Marianne North Gallery**
> *Open 09.30-16.00 (sometimes later in summer).* Admission charge for Kew Gardens includes Marianne North and Kew Gardens Gallery (see page 164).
> Shop. Guided tours. Guidebook.
> *Education facilities:* Tours for schools.
> &#x267f; No access
> &#x2296; Kew Gardens

## Narwhal Inuit Art Gallery

55 Linden Gardens, Chiswick W4. 081-747 1575.

Ken and Tija Mantel started collecting contemporary Inuit (Eskimo) art in the 1970s and put their collection on display in a basement gallery in their west London house in 1983. It consists of stone, whalebone and caribou horn carvings and graphic prints, and is the only one of its kind in the country. Most of the 400 or so pieces in the collection come from the Inuit of Canada, but there are a few items from Greenland as well.

---

**Narwhal Inuit Art Gallery**
*Open by appointment only Mon-Sun.* Admission free.
&#9855; No access
&#9035; Chiswick

---

## National Gallery

Trafalgar Square WC2. 071-839 3321.                    4 F3

The National Gallery houses Britain's national collection of Western European pictures painted during the seven centuries from the beginning of painting in Europe in the 13thC up to about 1920. Modern works are in the Tate Gallery. The Tate also contains most of the national collection of British pictures painted since our own native tradition began in the 16thC, but the National has retained a token but choice selection by some of the great 18thC and early 19thC masters: Turner, Hogarth, Gainsborough, Reynolds, Stubbs and Constable.

Begun by the purchase of 38 pictures from the estate of a deceased Russian *émigré* financier in 1824, the collection currently contains about 2200 pictures, many of them masterpieces known all over the world. The older masters are particularly well represented, with no less than 250 paintings from the Early Renaissance period between about 1260 (the start date for the collection) and 1510. With the exception of works out on loan or in conservation, all the pictures are on display at any one time in the Gallery's 70 rooms. Most of these are in the main building, originally designed by William Wilkins in 1832 but subsequently much-enlarged behind the scenes. The remainder are in the superb new Sainsbury Wing, completed in 1991 to designs by Venturi and Scott-Brown and funded by the Sainsbury supermarket family.

Traditionally the Gallery's pictures were hung by country of origin. But the entire collection has recently been rearranged in a broad chronological sequence so as to

*National Gallery*

emphasise the artistic links between painters of different nationalities working at roughly the same time. Hopefully this will make the individual pictures more meaningful.

If you want to find out more about any painting in the National Gallery, head for the Micro Gallery on the first floor of the Sainsbury Wing. Here a computerised, touch-screen, visual encyclopedia, which you operate yourself, contains detailed information on all the painters and paintings in the collection. Along with the re-hanging it makes this great art collection more accessible to more people than ever before.

Some of the most famous pictures in the Sainsbury Wing (with room numbers) are Leonardo's *Cartoon* (51); the *Wilton Diptych* (53); Uccello's *Battle of San Romano* (55); *The Arnolfini Marriage* by van Eyck (56); works by Botticelli (58) and Raphael (60). Highlights from the High Renaissance and later periods include Sebastiano del Piombo's *Raising of Lazarus* (8); Titian's *Bacchus and Ariadne* (9); works by Claude and Turner (15); *The Rokeby Venus* by Velázquez (29); 17thC State portraits by Rembrandt, Velázquez, Van Dyck and others (30); *The Supper at Emmaus* by Caravaggio (32) and *The Hay Wain* by Constable (35).

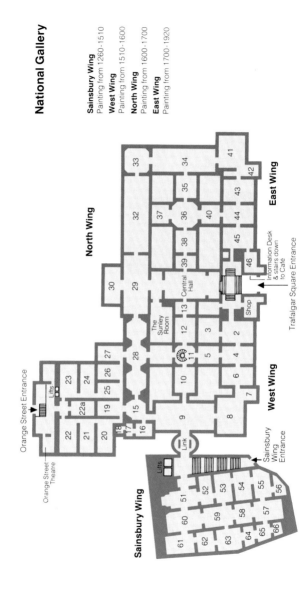

# National Gallery

**Sainsbury Wing**
Painting from 1260-1510

**West Wing**
Painting from 1510-1600

**North Wing**
Painting from 1600-1700

**East Wing**
Painting from 1700-1920

North Wing

East Wing

West Wing

Sainsbury Wing

Orange Street Entrance

Orange Street Theatre

Lifts

23

24

22a

19

22

21

20

18

17

16

15

25

26

27

28

30

29

The Sunley Room

13  13

12

11

10

9

5

3

2

4

6

7

8

Link

Lifts

51

52

53

54

55

56

60

59

58

57

61

62

63

64

65

66

Sainsbury Wing Entrance

32

33

34

37

36

35

38

39

40

41

42

43

44

45

46

Central Hall

Shop

Information Desk & stairs down to Cafe

Trafalgar Square Entrance

*Sainsbury Wing*

*Painting from 1260 to 1510*
51  Giotto, Leonardo
52  Italian before 1400
53  Italian before 1400; Wilton Diptych
54  Masaccio, Sassetta
55  Uccello, Pisanello
56  Campin, van Eyck, van der Weyden
57  Crivelli, Tura
58  Botticelli
59  Pollaiuolo, Piero di Cosimo
60  Raphael, Perugino
61  Bellini, Mantegna
62  Netherlandish and French
63  German
64  Netherlandish and Italian
65  Antonello, Bellini
66  Piero della Francesca

*North Wing*

*Painting from 1600 to 1700*
14  Claude, Poussin
15  Claude and Turner
16  Vermeer, de Hooch
17  Dou, van Mieris
18  Hoogstraten Peepshow
19  Dutch
20  Closed
21  Van Dyck, Jordaens
22  Rubens
22a French
23  Rubens, Teniers
24  Domenichino
25  Closed
26  Hals, Maes

27  Rembrandt
28  Dutch and French
29  Velázquez, Murillo, Zurbáran
30  State Portraits
32  Caravaggio, Reni, Giordano

*West Wing*

*Painting from 1510 to 1600*
2  Holbein, Cranach, Altdorfer
3  Closed
4  Pontormo, Dosso, Garfolo
5  Goassaert, Bruegel
6  Netherlandish
7  Tintoretto, El Greco
8  Michaelangelo, Sebastiano, Bronzino
9  Titian, Veronese, Tintoretto
10  Venetian
11  Veronese
12  Lotto, Moretto, Moroni
13  Closed

*East Wing*

*Painting from 1700 to 1920*
33  French
34  Italian and Spanish
35  Turner and Constable
36  British Portraits
37  Gainsborough and Wilson
38  Reynolds and Gainsborough
39  Hogarth, Stubbs
40  Delaroche, Whistler
41  Closed
42  Closed
43  Closed
44  van Gogh, Cézanne
45  Cézanne, Seurat, Picasso
46  Picasso

---

**National Gallery**
*Open 10.00-18.00 Mon-Sat, 14.00-18.00 Sun.* Admission free (except for loan exhibitions).
Shops. Guided tours. Guidebook. Films. Research facilities.
*Refreshments*: Licensed brasserie serving light and full meals. Café serving snacks. Both *open 10.00-17.00 Mon-Sat, 14.00-17.00 Sun.*
*Educational facilities*: Tours for schools, worksheets, lectures, workshops.
&#9855; Full access. Toilet.
&#9854; Charing Cross

## National Portrait Gallery

St Martin's Place WC2. 071-306 0055.                    4 F3

The National Portrait Gallery was founded in 1856 to collect likenesses of famous British men and women. The main building, behind the National Gallery, opened 40 years later, paid for by William Alexander, a wealthy property owner and benefactor of the arts. Originally living people were not accepted into the collection, but now they are and the Gallery actively encourages contemporary portrait painting by running an annual competition for young artists. Everybody who was (or is) anybody is here, including footballers and accountants as well as kings, queens, statesmen and soldiers. The gallery thus constitutes a visual dictionary of national biography from the time of the Tudors to the present day. One interesting way to view the collection is to pass quickly through the galleries, starting with the earliest. This will give you, quite literally, a moving picture show revealing changing fashions in dress and hairstyles, not to mention portraiture, over the past five centuries.

Currently the collection contains over 9000 portraits and that number is growing all the time. The majority are oil paintings, but there are also watercolours, drawings, miniatures, sculptures, caricatures, silhouettes and photographs. Only a relatively small proportion of the total is on show at any one time. The portraits are arranged chronologically, starting on the top floor, and then, within

*National Portrait Gallery*

# National Portrait Gallery

**Level 5** *(see overleaf)*

*Sixteenth Century*

1a Edward VI and Thomas More
1b Mary I
1c Elizabeth I

*Seventeenth Century*

2 James I and Charles I
3 17th Century Arts and Sciences
4 Charles II and James II
5 William & Mary and Queen Anne

*Eighteenth Century*

6 Early 18th Century Arts and Sciences
6a The Jacobites
7 The Kit-cat Club
8 George I and George II
9 18th Century Arts
10 The Struggle for America
11 Britain becomes a World Power

*Late Eighteenth Century and early Nineteenth Centuries*

12 Britain at war 1793–1815
12a Special Displays
13 The Romantics
14 Science and the Industrial Revolution
15 The Regency

**Level 3** *(see overleaf)*

16a Special Exhibitions

*The Victorians and Edwardians*

16 Science and Technology
17 Exploration and Empire
18 Victorian Drawings and Photographs
19 Politics and Public Life
20 Artists, Writers and Performers
21 The Portraits of G.F. Watts
22 Lecture Room
23 Politics and Public Life
24 Later Victorian Arts
25 The Edwardians
25a George V

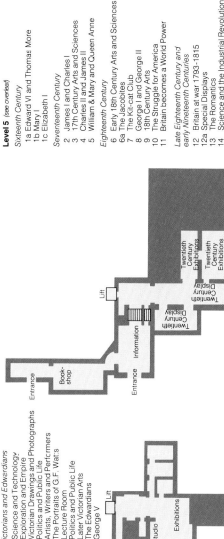

**Level 1**

Entrance
Book-shop
Lift
Information
Entrance
Twentieth Century Display
Twentieth Century Display
Twentieth Century Exhibitions
Twentieth Century Exhibitions

**Basement**

Lift
Studio
Exhibitions

# National Portrait Gallery

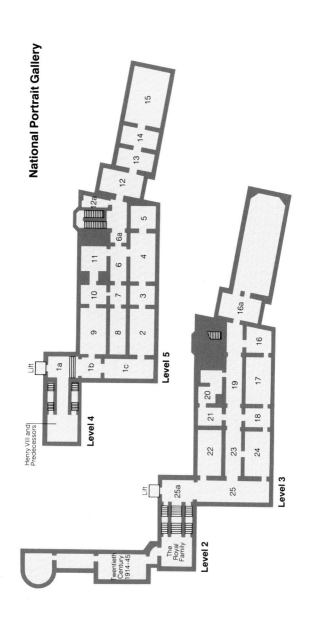

Henry VIII and
Predecessors

Lift

**Level 4**

1a
1b
1c

**Level 5**

9
10
11
12a
12
13
14
15
8
7
6
6a
2
3
4
5

**Level 3**

16a
16
17
18
19
20
21
22
23
24
25
25a

Lift

**Level 2**

Twentieth
Century
1914-45

The Royal
Family

each broad timespan, split into groups such as 17thC Arts and Sciences (Sir Isaac Newton, Thomas Hobbes and John Locke) or the Romantics (Byron, Keats and Shelley). The amount of space available for post-1945 portraits is obviously inadequate, but new galleries for modern works are planned to open in nearby Orange Street in 1993.

Many of the well-known historical pictures by top-rank artists like Holbein, Van Dyck, Reynolds, Gainsborough and Sargent will probably be more familiar to many visitors as period images than as portraits of recognisable people, so don't be surprised if you find yourself passing over them without a second thought. The contemporary likenesses, however, are a different matter. In fact they are positively arresting and, because they are proper portraits, tell us far more about a person in one viewing than a hundred casual sightings of the same face in the news media.

> **National Portrait Gallery**
> *Open 10.00-17.00 Mon-Fri, 10.00-18.00 Sat, 14.00-18.00 Sun.*
> Admission free (except for special exhibitions).
> Shop. Guided tours. Guidebook. Films. Research facilities.
> *Educational facilities*: Tours for schools, worksheets, lectures, workshops.
> ♿ Partial access. Toilet.
> ⊖ Charing Cross

## The Queen's Gallery

Buckingham Palace Road SW1. 071-930 4832.     4 C5

Opened in 1962 on the site of a chapel destroyed by bombing in World War II, the one-room Queen's Gallery at Buckingham Palace holds regular public exhibitions of art treasures from the otherwise private royal collection. This collection, built up over centuries, is so large that even after 25 exhibitions, things are still being shown that have never been seen in public before. At the same time the collection's range and depth is such that the gallery has been able to devote entire exhibitions to individual artists, including Leonardo da Vinci, Van Dyck, Gainsborough, Holbein and Canaletto, and to individual subjects as diverse as stamps, Sèvres porcelain, old master drawings and Fabergé jewellery.

> **The Queen's Gallery**
> *Open 10.00-17.00 Tue-Sat & Bank Hols, 14.00-17.00 Sun.*
> Admission charge.
> Shop. Sound guide.
> *Educational facilities*: Tours for schools.
> ♿ Partial access. Toilet.
> ⊖ Green Park, Victoria, Hyde Park

**Royal Academy of Arts**

Burlington House, Piccadilly W1. 071-439 7438.        4 D3

Founded in 1768, the Royal Academy is the oldest and most prestigious fine arts institution in Britain. For well over a century it has been based in Burlington House, an 18thC nobleman's town house in a courtyard off Piccadilly. This setting combines traditional galleries with an ultra-modern exhibition space in the form of the Sackler Galleries, designed by Norman Foster and opened in 1991. As you ascend to these top-floor galleries (by stairs or glass-sided lift) you can see the old garden front of Burlington House, sadly no longer facing gardens.

The Academy is best known for its loan exhibitions and annual Summer Exhibition. The Summer Exhibition (June-August) is open to all artists and is the most popular of its kind in the country. There are usually about 1200 works on show – paintings, drawings, prints, sculpture, architectural models and drawings – and most of them are for sale. In addition, up to six loan exhibitions are held each year. Historical and contemporary, British and foreign, they are major scholarly events of international significance and often draw huge crowds.

Not so well-known is the fact that the RA also has its own permanent collection. This has been built up largely as a result of deposits by Academicians on taking their diplomas. It therefore includes works by most leading British artists of the last two centuries – Gainsborough, Reynolds, Turner, Constable, Lawrence and Sargent to name but a few. There are also some foreign works – given, bequeathed or acquired for use in the RA schools (the Academy is also involved in arts education). Exhibitions based on the permanent collection are held in the Private Rooms of the Academy. The works on show change, but the theme is generally the history of the Academy.

Two very special works from the permanent collection are always on display: one is a contemporary copy of Leonardo's Last Supper, the best of several in existence (in the Private Rooms); the other is Michelangelo's marble relief or tondo of *The Virgin and Child with the Infant St John* (near the entrance to the Sackler Galleries and adjacent to the sculpture promenade). One of only four of Michelangelo's carvings outside Italy, this is the Academy's most prized possession.

**Royal Academy of Arts**
*Open 10.00-18.00 Mon-Sun.* Admission charge. Private Rooms
*open 10.00-16.00 Tue-Sun.* Admission free.
Shop. Sound guides. Films. Research facilities.
*Refreshments*: Restaurant serving hot & cold meals from a
changing menu. Coffee shop serving drinks, sandwiches and
pastries. Both *open 10.00-18.00 Mon-Sun.*
*Educational facilities*: Tours for schools, worksheets, lectures,
workshops.
&#x267f; Full access. Toilet.
&#x2296; Piccadilly

## Royal College of Music Department of Portraits

Prince Consort Road SW7. 071-589 3643.                    3 E6
Since its foundation in 1883, the Royal College of Music has
built up the largest international collection of music-related
portraits in the country. With some items dating back to the
17thC, there are sculptures, photographs and thousands of
prints as well as oil paintings and watercolours. The collection
features not only musicians and composers, but also musical
publishers, dancers, instrument makers, in fact anybody in
any way connected with music anywhere in the world. The
paintings and sculpture are displayed in a small gallery in the
West Tower of the College. Some of the picture highlights are
*Haydn* by Thomas Hardy (1790), *Weber* by John Cawse
(1826) and *Paderewski* by Burne-Jones (1890).

The Royal College of Music also has a Museum of
Instruments (see page 77).

**Royal College of Music Department of Portraits**
*Open during term by appointment.* Admission free.
Guided tours. Research facilities.
*Educational facilities*: Tours for schools, lectures.
&#x267f; No access
&#x2296; Knightsbridge (then bus 9, 10, 52, 52A), South Kensington (then
bus 49, C1)

## Royal College of Physicians

11 St Andrew's Place, Regent's Park NW1.                  1 D5
071-935 1174 x 374.
Since its foundation in 1518 the Royal College of Physicians
has built up a portrait collection of about 350 paintings,
miniatures and busts of past Fellows and other medical and
scientific personalities dating from the 16thC to the present
day. The pictures are hung around the walls of the College's

modern building near Regent's Park. They include some fine works by Lely, Kneller, Reynolds, Zoffany and Lawrence, but by and large they are more important historically than artistically.

---

**Royal College of Physicians**
*Open by appointment only 09.30-17.30 Mon-Fri.* Admission free.
Guided tours. Research facilities.
🚫 No access
⊖ Regent's Park

---

## Saatchi Collection

98a Boundary Road, St John's Wood NW8. 071-624 8299.
This private art collection was formed by Charles Saatchi, one of the founding brothers of the famous advertising agency. It contains about 800 paintings and sculptures produced over the last 25 years and is one of the largest such collections in the world. Most of the works are by British and American artists, Warhol, Freud, Twombly, Stella and Auerbach being particularly well represented. The collection is displayed by means of two exhibitions a year in the Saatchi Gallery, a converted motor repair shop built in the 1920s. Each exhibition features three or four artists at a time.

---

**Saatchi Collection**
*Open 12.00-18.00 Fri-Sat.* Admission free.
🚹 Full access except for difficult entrance steps.
⊖ St John's Wood

---

*Saatchi Collection*

**Tate Gallery**
Millbank SW1. 071-821 1313.                    7 E2

The Tate is a national gallery containing two great art collections. The first is British art from about 1550 to the present day, mainly paintings up to c1900 and, thereafter, paintings and sculpture. All the great names are present: Hilliard, Hogarth, Reynolds, Gainsborough, Constable, Rossetti, Burne-Jones, Sargent, Spencer, Bacon and Henry Moore. Blake and Turner are also well represented: Blake by over 150 watercolours, drawings and prints; Turner by the 300 oil paintings and 20,000 works on paper in the Turner Bequest, the pictures he left to the nation when he died in 1851.

The Tate's second major collection is of international 20thC painting and sculpture. Starting with Impressionism and Cézanne, Gauguin, and van Gogh, this traces the development of art abroad through Matisse, Picasso, Braque and movements like Futurism, Surrealism and Pop Art right up to the present day. Holdings of works by Mark Rothko, Naum Gabo and the sculptor Alberto Giacommetti are especially strong.

The Turner collection is displayed in the specially built Clore Gallery, tacked on to the side of the main building and opened in 1987. All the oils are on view in the main or reserve galleries. Changing exhibitions show selections of his works on paper.

The rest of the Tate's contents are displayed in the main building, given to the nation by sugar refiner Sir Henry Tate, along with his contemporary British art collection, in 1897. Tate's building, designed by Sidney Smith, was later extended three times thanks to the generosity of the Duveen family of art dealers. A simple chronological arrangement traces, first, the evolution of British art from the Tudors to Impressionism, and then the inter-relationship of British and foreign art through the schools of Paris, New York and now continental Europe. Within the overall sequence, changing displays bring out individual artists or special themes in more depth.

Because the Tate holds such a vast number of works, it has to rotate its displays, so that only part of its collection is on show at any one time. This makes it rather difficult to give a reliable breakdown of the contents of each room (of which there are over 30), but the Tate produces a new *plan* for each new display year, so the best policy is to pick one up as you go in. The Information Desk will be pleased to tell you where to see specific pictures. If they are not on display, you can make an appointment for a one-hour visit to the store.

**Tate Gallery**
*Open 10.00-17.50 Mon-Sat, 14.00-17.50 Sun*. Admission free
(except for major loan exhibitions).
Shop. Guided tours. Films. Research facilities.
*Refreshments*: Excellent licensed restaurant serving traditional
British food *12.00-15.00 Mon-Sat*. Coffee shop, serving drinks,
sandwiches, cakes and cold meals *10.30-17.30 Mon & Wed-Sat,
11.00-17.30 Tue, 14.00-17.00 Sun*.
*Educational facilities*: Tours for schools, lectures.
&#9855; Full access. Toilet.
&#9758; Pimlico

## Thomas Coram Foundation for Children

40 Brunswick Square WC1. 071-278 2424.                   1 G5
This 250-year-old charitable foundation, set up by Captain
Thomas Coram to care for abandoned children, has a large
collection of paintings, sculpture and other works of art. They
were mainly given in the 18thC by the artists themselves as a
way of attracting visitors, and therefore funds, to the
Foundling Hospital. William Hogarth, an early governor of
the Hospital, started the tradition with his fine portrait of
Coram, painted in 1740. Other 18thC British artists represented in the collection – not always at their best it has to be said
– include Gainsborough, Reynolds, Allan Ramsay, Highmore,
Hudson, Copley, Benjamin West, Roubiliac and Rysbrack.
One of the greatest treasures in the collection is the largest
surviving cartoon for the *Scuola Nuova* tapestry in the
Vatican, painted in the studio of Raphael.
   Also on show are a model of the Foundling Hospital,
demolished in 1926, various Hospital relics like the old-fashioned uniforms worn by the girls and boys until the 1950s;
letters from famous people like Dickens and Admiral Lord
Nelson, and the keyboard of the organ donated by Handel on
which he performed his annual fund-raising concerts. Most
of the collection is displayed in the Court Room and
Picture Gallery, two fine rooms removed from the original
18thC Hospital and re-erected in the Foundation's 20thC
headquarters.

**Thomas Coram Foundation for Children**
*Open 10.00-16.00 Mon-Fri, but subject to alteration. Phone to
check*. Admission charge.
Shop. Guided tours.
&#9855; No access
&#9758; Russell Square

## Wallace Collection

Hertford House, Manchester Square W1. 071-935 0687.     4 B1

This huge collection of works of art of the highest quality was amassed in the 19thC by the 3rd and 4th Marquesses of Hertford and the 4th Marquess's illegitimate son, Sir Richard Wallace. Wallace's widow gave the collection, by now world-famous, to the nation in 1897. Since 1900 it has been displayed in 25 sumptuous rooms on the ground and first floors of what was the family's palatial town house-cum-museum just north of Oxford Street. Built around a courtyard, much of Hertford House was constructed specifically to house the collection, so it is really much more of a museum that the family home you might have expected – even a palatial one – and certainly has that museum atmosphere.

The 4th Marquess spent much of his life in Paris, which helps to explain why the collection is dominated by French works of art; paintings, furniture, clocks and china, mainly of the 18thC. The quality of these objects is absolutely outstanding. The Sèvres porcelain is the finest in any museum in the world. Much of the furniture was made by leading cabinet-makers like André-Charles Boulle for the royal palaces of Versailles, the Petit Trianon, Fontainebleau and St Cloud. Among the paintings are some of the finest works by Boucher, Fragonard and Watteau. Gallery 21 is the centre-piece of the French collection. You will not see a finer group of 18thC French furniture and painting in a single room anywhere else in the world. One of the highlights of this room is Fragonard's famous picture of *The Swing* showing a girl on a swing admired by a young man reclining in the bushes.

The main gallery in the museum is the top-lit No 19. One of the finest picture galleries in the world, it houses 70 paintings. The majority date from the mid-17thC and include works by Rembrandt, Rubens, Van Dyck, Velázquez, Murillo, Poussin and Claude. Also on show here are some superb Titians; 18thC English portraits by Gainsborough, Reynolds and their contemporaries; and Dutch pictures, including *The Laughing Cavalier* by Frans Hals, the most famous picture in the collection. Indeed the 17thC Dutch and Flemish pictures are one of the main strengths of the whole Wallace collection.

Other important contents, listed in the location guide below, include one of the world's finest arms and armour collections (and the best in England outside the Tower of London); two rooms of 18thC views of Venice by Canaletto and Guardi; 300 portrait miniatures; magnificent gold snuff boxes; early Italian paintings and bronzes; and medieval and Renaissance works of art.

|  | *Ground Floor* | *First Floor* |
|---|---|---|
| 18thC French painting | Grand Staircase | 21, 22, 25 |
| 19thC French painting | 2 | 19, 20 |
| 18thC French furniture | 1, 2, 11, 12 | 13, 14, 21, 22, 24, 25 |
| Sèvres porcelain | 2, 12 | 14 |
| 17thC Dutch and Flemish painting |  | 15-18 |
| 17thC European painting | 2 | 19 |
| Canaletto and Guardi |  | 13, 14 |
| 18thC and 19thC English portraits | 1 | 19 |
| Paintings by Bonington, Delaroche and Delacroix | 10 |  |
| Early Italian and medieval and Renaissance works of art | 3, 4 |  |
| Arms and Armour (Oriental) | 5-7, (8) |  |
| Miniatures |  | 20, 21 |
| Gold snuff boxes |  | Corridor between 23 and 24 |

**Wallace Collection**
*Open 10.00-17.00 Mon-Sat, 14.00-17.00 Sun.* Admission free.
Shop. Guided tours. Research facilities.
Educational facilities: Tours for schools, lectures.
♿ Full access. Toilet.
⊖ Bond Street

# EXHIBITION GALLERIES

*Note*: Some of the galleries listed below have their own permanent collections, but have been included here because they are primarily known as venues for temporary loan exhibitions, and only show works from their own collections on an occasional basis.

## Accademia Italiana Delle Arti e Delle Arti Applicate

24 Rutland Gate SW7. 071-225 3474.          3 F6

Opened in 1989, this gallery specialises in exhibitions of Italian art. It shows work in all media, and from all periods of Italian history, from Roman times to the present day. It also exhibits works of art which may not have been produced by Italians but which nevertheless have some Italian connection – Italian landscapes by foreign artists for example. Café (small entrance fee for non-friends of the Accademia), shop, limited visitor services. *Open 10.00-17.30 Tue & Thur-Sat, 10.00-20.00 Wed, 14.00-17.30 Sun.* Admission charge (free one day a week – phone for details).

Ⓖ Partial access

⊖ Knightsbridge

## Architectural Association

36 Bedford Square WC1. 071-636 0974.          1 F6

Founded in 1847 and a combination of learned society, club and school of architecture, the AA mounts regular changing exhibitions with architectural themes. Normally works by professional architects rather than artists. Café, shop. *Open during exhibitions 09.00-18.00 Mon-Fri, 09.00-15.00 Sat.* Admission free.

Ⓖ Partial access – main hall only.

⊖ Goodge Street

## Association of Illustrators

1 Colville Place, off Charlotte Street W1.          1 F6
071-636 4100.

Founded in 1973 to promote professional standards in the industry and to represent its members, the AOI has a small exhibition space at its office near the Tottenham Court Road. There is always an exhibition here, whether it be a member show, an exhibition by an invited artist, or an art college degree show. The illustrations cover a wide range, including cartoons, prints, book illustrations and photographs. Usually all works are for sale, and they are cheaper and more fun than fine art. *Open 10.00-18.00 Mon-Fri.* Admission free.

&#9855; Partial access. Toilet.

&#8854; Knightsbridge

### Bankside Gallery

48 Hopton Street SE1. 071-928 7521.                    5 C4

Opened in 1980 on the south bank of the Thames opposite St Paul's, the Bankside Gallery is the shared home of two prestigious 19thC art societies: the Royal Watercolour Society (RWS) and the Royal Society of Painter-Etchers and Engravers (RE). Between them the societies host 10 exhibitions a year, the main ones being the spring and autumn shows of the RWS, the annual show of the RE, and the RWS Summer Exhibition, open to all watercolour artists in the UK. Works at these exhibitions are generally for sale. The gallery also mounts loan exhibitions. Shop. *Open during exhibitions 10.00-20.00 Tue, 10.00-17.00 Wed-Sat, 13.00-17.00 Sun.* Admission charge.

&#9855; Full access. Toilet.

&#8854; Blackfriars

### Barbican Art Gallery

Level 8, Barbican Centre, Silk Street EC2.            2 E6
071-588 9023.

Part of the modern Barbican Arts Centre opened in 1982, this is the City of London's art gallery and one of the largest and

*Barbican Arts Centre*

most imaginative in London. It mounts regular exhibitions of photography, video, posters, graphics and paintings (mainly 19thC and 20thC), mixing popular shows with more challenging and innovatory ones. Cafés, shop. *Open 10.00-18.45 Mon & Wed-Sat, 10.00-17.45 Tue, 12.00-18.45 Sun & Bank Hols.* Admission charge (cheap tickets on *Thur from 17.00*).

&#x267F; Full access. Toilet.

&#x2296; Barbican

### Ben Uri Art Society
4th Floor, 21 Dean Street W1. 071-437 2852.  4 E2
Founded in the East End in 1915 to promote Anglo-Jewish cultural life, this Jewish art society puts on regular exhibitions of new and established Jewish artists and covers general themes of Jewish interest. It also holds an annual autumn open exhibition, and each year mounts one special exhibition based on its own permanent collection. This numbers over 500 paintings, sculptures, prints and drawings, and includes works by leading Jewish artists such as Frank Auerbach, Josef Herman, Max Liebermann, Jacob Epstein and David Bomberg. Bomberg's *Ghetto Theatre* is probably the most famous work in the collection. Plans are in hand to provide the collection with a permanent display area. *Open 10.00-17.00 Mon-Thur, 14.00-17.00 occasional Sun (phone for details).* Admission free to most exhibitions.

&#x267F; Full access

&#x2296; Tottenham Court Road

### Building Centre Gallery
26 Store Street WC1. 071-637 1022.  4 E1
A bookshop and information point housed in the Building Centre, specialising in building design and construction, the Building Centre Gallery holds about 10 exhibitions a year. Some are technical, befitting the Centre's function, some are artistic, but all have a broadly architectural theme. Shop. *Open 09.30-17.00 Mon-Fri, 10.00-13.00 Sat.* Admission free.

&#x267F; Full access. Toilet.

&#x2296; Goodge Street

### Café Gallery
By the Pool, Southwark Park, Bermondsey SE16.
071-232 2170.
Opened in 1984 and run by the Bermondsey Artists Group, the gallery acts as a showcase for both fine art and the work

of local community groups. Café, shop. *Open 10.00-17.00 Wed-Sun*. Admission free.
&#x267F; Full access
&#x2296; Surrey Quays

## Camden Arts Centre
Arkwright Road, Hampstead NW3. 071-435 2643/5224.
The exhibition gallery in this multi-activity arts centre holds between six and eight contemporary art exhibitions a year, primarily of painting and sculpture. Bookshop. *Open 12.00-20.00 Tue-Thur, 12.00-18.00 Fri-Sun*. Admission free.
&#x267F; No access
&#x2296; Finchley Road

## Canada House Gallery
Canada House, Trafalgar Square SW1. 071-629 9492.      4 F4
Gallery in the Canadian High Commission showing changing exhibitions of Canadian contemporary, historical and folk art. *Open 11.00-17.00 Mon-Fri*. Admission free.
&#x267F; Partial access. Toilet.
&#x2296; Charing Cross

## Chisenhale Gallery
64-84 Chisenhale Road, Bow E3. 081-981 4518.
Opened in 1986, he Chisenhale Gallery holds regular changing exhibitions of innovative contemporary or experimental art. Sculpture and installation are specialities. *Open 13.00-18.00 Wed-Sun*. Admission free.
&#x267F; Partial access. Toilet.
&#x2296; Mile End (then bus 8, 277)

## Contemporary Applied Arts
43 Earlham Street WC2. 071-836 6993.      4 E2
A combined gallery and shop showing and selling innovative craft work in ceramics, jewellery, glass, wood, textiles, furniture and metal. The work is produced by artist-members of the Contemporary Applied Arts organisation. Shop. *Open 10.00-17.30 Mon-Sat*. Admission free.
&#x267F; Partial access – ground floor only.
&#x2296; Covent Garden

## Craft Shop and Gallery
Royal Festival Hall, Belvedere Road SE1.      4 G4
071-928 3002.
A combined shop and gallery in the foyer of the Royal Festival Hall (see page 167) which mounts monthly exhibi-

tions of modern craft work by British artists and designers. Cafés and restaurants in Royal Festival Hall. *Open 12.30-19.30 Mon-Sun.* Admission free.

&#x267F; Full access. Toilet.

&#x2296; Embankment, Waterloo

### Crafts Council

44a Pentonville Road N1. 071-278 7700.   2 B3

Set up in 1971 to help craftspeople in England and Wales establish workshops and sell their work, the Crafts Council has a gallery here at its headquarters where it mounts between four and six craft exhibitions a year, mainly of British work. Some exhibitions include pieces which are for sale. Café, shop. *Open 11.00-18.00 Tue-Sat, 14.00-18.00 Sun.* Admission free.

&#x267F; Full access

&#x2296; South Kensington

### Galerie Matisse

Institut Français, 17 Queensberry Place SW7.   6 D2
071-589 6211.

The gallery of the French Institute in London mounts regular exhibitions, featuring works by both new and established French artists or art with a French theme. Café. *Open 10.00-19.00 Mon-Fri.*

&#x267F; Full access

&#x2296; South Kensington

### Goethe-Institut

50 Princes Gate, Exhibition Road SW7. 071-581 3344.   6 D1

The cultural presence of Germany in London, the Goethe-Institut has its own gallery in which it regularly exhibits works of art by living German artists, or works, perhaps as part of an historical exhibition, with a German theme. Café. *Open 10.00-18.00 Mon-Thur, 10.00-16.00 Fri, 10.00-12.30 Sat.* Admission free.

&#x267F; No access

&#x2296; Knightsbridge (then bus 9, 10, 52, 52A), South Kensington (then bus 49, C1)

### Goldsmiths' Hall

Foster Lane EC2. 071-606 7010.   5 D2

The headquarters of the Goldsmiths' Livery Company in the City. The company actively supports modern jewellery-making and silversmithing. It holds about four exhibitions a year in its magnificent Livery Hall, which is not otherwise open to the public. Two are regular events: the Goldsmiths Fair in the autumn, when over 70 designer makers display and sell their pieces to the public; and the Passing Out Exhibition in December, a degree-work show by jewellery and silver-smithing students. The other two exhibitions are generally one-man shows or retrospectives featuring the work of individual designers or design houses. *Open during exhibitions 10.00-17.00 Mon-Fri*. Admission usually free.

&#x267F; Partial access

&#x2296; St Paul's

## Hayward Gallery

South Bank Centre SE1. 071-928 3144.                          5 A4

A major international venue for art exhibitions, historical and contemporary, individual and thematic. Showing contem-porary British art is an important part of the Gallery's programme. The gallery is easily recognisable within the South Bank complex because of the colourful kinetic sculpture on top of the building. Café, shop. *Open during exhibitions 10.00-18.00 Mon-Sun (to 20.00 Tue & Wed)*. Admission charge.

&#x267F; Full access. Toilet.

&#x2296; Waterloo, Embankment

## Institute of Contemporary Arts

The Mall SW1. 071-930 0493.                          4 E4

Since its foundation in 1948 the ICA has grown into one of the most innovative arts institutions in the world. Among a whole host of activities, it mounts about 12 art exhibitions a year covering ground-breaking contemporary and 20thC art in all media and from all countries. At its monthly Talking Art event, artists from home and abroad appear in person and talk about their work. Café, shop. *Open 12.00-22.00 Mon-Sat, 12.00-21.00 Sun*. Admission charge for non-members.

&#x267F; Partial access

&#x2296; Charing Cross, Piccadilly Circus

## Kew Gardens Gallery

Royal Botanic Gardens, Kew, Richmond, Surrey.
081-940 1171.

Cambridge Cottage, an 18thC house used by Royal Dukes of Cambridge in the 19thC, is one of several buildings in Kew Gardens and today provides space for the Kew Gardens Gallery. This modern gallery mounts regular exhibitions of botanical illustrations and flower paintings. Some exhibitions include works which are for sale. Shop. *Open 09.30-16.00*

*Kew Gardens Gallery*

*(sometimes later).* Admission charge for Kew Gardens includes the Marianne North Gallery (see page 143).
&#x267F; Full access. Toilet.
&#x2296; Kew Gardens

## Mall Galleries
The Mall SW1. 071-930 6844.                    4 E4
The home of nine art societies which together make up the Federation of British Artists. The societies are: the Royal Societies of Portrait Painters, Marine Artists and British Artists; the Royal Institutes of Oil Painters and Painters in Water Colours; the Society of Wildlife Artists; the Pastel Society; the New English Art Club, and the Hesketh Hubbard Art Society.
   The gallery shows the annual exhibitions of all its member societies, plus a changing programme of other exhibitions, often put on by outside organisations which hire the gallery space. *Open 10.00-17.00 Mon-Sun.* Admission charge, sometimes free.
&#x267F; No access
&#x2296; Charing Cross, Piccadilly Circus

## The Orangery and Ice House
Holland Park W8. 071-602 7344.                    3 A5
Formerly the outbuildings of Holland House – a famous coun-

try mansion badly bomb-damaged in the last war and later acquired by the local council – these two galleries are now used for all kinds of art exhibitions, some mounted by artists themselves. *Open during exhibitions Mar-Oct 11.00-19.00 Mon-Sun.* Admission free.

&#x267F; Full access. Toilet.

&#x2296; Holland Park

## Orleans House Gallery

Riverside, Twickenham, Middlesex. 081-892 0221.

A varied exhibition programme including Arts Council touring exhibitions, historical and biographical exhibitions, shows by local artists and photographers, the work of local schools and colleges, and selections from the Gallery's two permanent collections: the Richmond and Twickenham Borough Art Collection, and the Ionides Collection of 18thC and 19thC local portraits and topographical views.

The gallery stands in a woodland garden near the Thames and incorporates the octagon (designed by James Gibbs) of an 18thC mansion pulled down in the 1920s. The mansion acquired its curious name in the last century from the Duc d'Orléans, leader of the French royalist *émigrés* in Britain, who lived here from 1815-1817. Later he ruled France as King Louis Philippe from 1830-48. *Open Apr-Sep 13.00-17.30 Tue-Sat, 14.00-17.30 Sun & Bank Hols (Oct-Mar to 16.30) Mon-Sun.* Admission free.

&#x267F; Partial access. Toilet.

&#x2740; St Margaret's

## Photographers' Gallery

5 & 8 Great Newport Street WC2. 071-831 1771.          4 E3

Opened in 1971, this was the first independent gallery in Britain devoted entirely to photography at a professional level. It holds 21 exhibitions a year, mainly new work but sometimes historical or thematic. Budding photographers are welcome to bring their own work along for a professional opinion *18.00-19.00 Tue-Fri.* Café, shop. *Open 11.00-19.00 Tue-Sat.* Admission free.

&#x267F; Full access. Toilet.

&#x2296; Leicester Square

## Riverside Studios Gallery

Crisp Road, Hammersmith W6. 081-748 3354.

Part of the riverside arts centre in Hammersmith, this gallery shows regular exhibitions of contemporary art in all media

and at all levels, from local to international. *Open 13.00-20.00 Tue-Sun.* Admission free.
&#9855; Full access. Toilet.
&#9727; Hammersmith

### Royal College of Art Exhibition Galleries
Kensington Gore SW7. 071-584 5020.　　　　3 E5
The Royal College of Art is a postgraduate school of art and design, and holds two degree shows a year. At other times the galleries are hired by many different organisations who mount a wide range of exhibitions in all media. Café, shop. *Open during exhibitions 10.00-18.00 Mon-Fri.* Admission usually free.
&#9855; Full access. Toilet.
&#9727; High Street Kensington

### Royal Festival Hall
Belvedere Road SE1. 071-928 3002.　　　　4 G4
This famous concert hall was built in the 1950s as part of the South Bank development for the Festival of Britain. Its large foyer, also containing shops, bars and cafés, is used for art exhibitions, contemporary and historical, in all media. The most important are the two annual South Bank 'opens', one for painting (December-January) and one for photographs

*Royal Festival Hall*

(May-June). Cafés, bars and restaurants. Shop. *Open 10.00-22.00 Mon-Sun*. Admission free.

&#x267F; Full access. Toilet.

&#x2296; Embankment, Waterloo

## Royal Institute of British Architects (RIBA)

66 Portland Place W1. 071-580 5533.                    4 C1

Part club, part learned society and part professional association, the RIBA, founded in 1834, has a gallery in its West End headquarters which it uses to exhibit contemporary artwork in different media, sometimes, but not always, with an architectural theme. Bookshop. *Open during exhibitions 10.00-17.30 Mon-Fri, 10.00-13.00 Sat*. Admission free.

&#x267F; Full access. Toilet.

&#x2296; Great Portland Street

## Serpentine Gallery

Kensington Gardens W2. 071-402 6075.                  3 E4

A former tea pavilion, this charming little building in Kensington Gardens has been used by the Arts Council for exhibitions of mainly British contemporary art since 1972. There are four naturally-lit main rooms and a lawn outside for sculpture and performing arts events. Shop. *Open during exhibitions 10.00-18.00 Mon-Sun*. Admission free.

&#x267F; Full access. Toilet.

&#x2296; Knightsbridge, Lancaster Gate

## The Showroom

44 Bonner Road, Bethnal Green E2. 081-983 4115.

Up to eight exhibitions a year featuring innovative contemporary art in the fields of sculpture, installation, paintings, photography and performance. Occasionally works are for sale. *Open 13.00-18.00 Thur-Sun*. Admission free.

&#x267F; Full access

&#x2744; Cambridge Heath

## Small Mansion Art Gallery

Gunnersbury Park, Pope's Lane, Acton W3. 081-993 8312.

Here and at the nearby Orangery, the artist-run Small Mansion Arts Centre mounts regular exhibitions in different media, often of local community interest. The 'small mansion' is a Regency country house close to a larger house of similar date which now houses the Gunnersbury Park local history museum (see page 173). Until 1926 both houses and the surrounding parkland were owned by the Rothschild

*Small Mansion Art Gallery*

family. Usually *open 13.00-17.00 Tue-Sun, but times vary so phone to check.* Admission free.
&#9855; Full access. Toilet.
&#8854; Acton Town (then bus E3)

### South London Art Gallery

65 Peckham Road, Camberwell SE5. 071-703 6120.
This historic art gallery was founded in 1891 and has close artistic (and geographical) links with the famous Camberwell School of Art. Primarily an exhibitions venue, it holds between four and six exhibitions a year, some featuring the work of local artists. It also puts on occasional shows of work from its own permanent collection. Otherwise in store, but available for viewing on request, the collection spans some 200 years and includes fine pictures by famous artists such as Millais, Prinsep, Ruskin, Sutherland and Spencer, and paintings and drawings depicting the history and social life of the borough of Southwark. Shop. *Open during exhibitions 10.00-18.00 Tue-Fri (to 20.00 Thur), 15.00-18.00 Sun.* Admission free.
&#9855; Partial access
&#8854; Elephant & Castle (then bus 12, 171, P3)

### Westminster Gallery

Westminster Central Hall, Storey's Gate SW1.     4 E5
071-222 2723.
Lettable gallery space in the basement of the Methodist Central Hall near Westminster Abbey. Art societies such as

the Royal Miniature Society, the Society of Equestrian
Artists, the Medical Art Society and the British Sporting Art
Trust regularly use it for their annual shows. Café. *Open during exhibitions 10.00-17.00 Mon-Sun.* Admission usually free.
&#9855; Partial access. Toilet.
&#1012; Westminster

## Whitechapel Art Gallery

80-82 Whitechapel High Street E1. 071-377 0107.          5 G2
An internationally famous art gallery with a reputation for
pioneering exhibitions of modern and contemporary art.
Founded in 1901 to bring major works of art to the people of
east London, it also shows work produced by the flourishing
local artists community, notably in its annual Open. There are
said to be more artists living and working in the East End of
London than in any other city in Europe. Café, shop. *Open
11.00-17.00 Tue-Sun (to 20.00 Wed).* Admission free, except
for special exhibitions.
&#9855; Full access. Toilet.
&#1012; Aldgate East

## Woodlands Art Gallery

90 Mycenae Road, Blackheath SE3. 081-858 5847.
The most important exhibition space in south-east London,
this independent gallery holds monthly exhibitions of paintings, prints, photography, sculpture, textiles, jewellery and
ceramics, often by local people. It has four rooms on the
ground floor of an 18thC country villa built for financier and
founder of Lloyd's, John Julius Angerstein – the man whose
picture collection formed the basis of the National Gallery.
The upper floor is used by the Greenwich Local History
Library. Shop. *Open 11.00-17.00 Mon-Sat, 14.00-17.00 Sun.*
Admission free.
&#9855; Partial access. Toilet.
&#10118; Westcombe Park

# LOCAL HISTORY MUSEUMS

Especially interesting for people who live in London are the 30-plus local history museums dotted around the outlying parts of the capital. What makes them all the more attractive is that they are often located in old country houses or other historic buildings such as tithe barns and canalside warehouses. These local history museums generally contain the same kinds of exhibits and cover the same broad subjects so they have all been grouped together and have not been given individual descriptions. We do, however, mention unusual collections or exhibits which you might not expect to find. We have also indicated if the museum is housed in an historic or otherwise interesting building, and what area it covers if it is not obvious from its name.

## Barnet Museum
31 Wood Street, Barnet, Hertfordshire. 081-440 8066. Fine Victorian, Edwardian and 20thC costume collection. Shop, limited visitor services. *Open 14.30-16.30 Tue-Thur, 10.00-12.00 & 14.30-16.30 Sat*. Admission free.
&#x267F; Partial access – ground floor only.
&#x2296; High Barnet

## Bexley Museum
Hall Place, Bourne Road, Bexley, Kent. (0322) 526574. 16thC and 17thC country house set in landscaped gardens and grounds. Along with Erith Museum below, covers the London borough of Bexley. Café, shop, limited visitor services, limited educational facilities. *Open Apr-Oct 10.00-17.00 Mon-Sat, 14.00-18.00 Sun; Nov-Mar 10.00-16.00 Mon-Sat*. Admission free.
&#x267F; No access
&#x2733; Bexley Village

## Bromley Museum
The Priory, Church Hill, Orpington, Kent. (0689) 873826. Medieval priory converted into a country house in the 17thC. Covers the London borough of Bromley. Shop, limited visitor services. *Open 09.00-17.00 Mon-Wed, Fri & Sat*. Admission free.
&#x267F; Partial access. Toilet.
&#x2733; Orpington

## Bruce Castle Museum

Lordship Lane, Tottenham N17. 081-808 8772. Former manor
house of Tottenham, built in the 16thC. Covers the London
borough of Haringey. Includes the *Riches of the East* gallery
telling the story of Haringey's links with British trade and
empire in India; an important postal history collection; and
the regimental museum of the Middlesex Regiment.
Refreshments vending machines, shop, full visitor services,
limited educational facilities. *Open 13.00-17.00 Tue-Sun.*
Admission free.

& Partial access – ground floor only.

⊖ Wood Green

## Cuming Museum

155-157 Walworth Road, Walworth SE17. 071-701 1342.
Museum for the London borough of Southwark. As well as
important local history displays, it also houses the Cuming
Collection, an incredible miscellany of 100,000 objects illustrating, like a mini British Museum, the progress of civiliza-
tion all over the world since the days of ancient Egypt.
Collected over a period of 120 years by Richard Cuming and
his son Henry, whose bequest led to the founding of the
Cuming Museum in 1906.

The Cuming has another important and unique collection –
this time of London superstitions and charms. Put together by
bank cashier Edward Lovett around the turn of the century, it
includes such curiosities as a whelk with a left-hand spiral in
its shell, worn as a good luck charm during World War I.
Although it used to be on show, the collection is now normally kept in store but access can be arranged if you are interested. Full visitor services, limited educational facilities. *Open
10.00-17.00 Tue-Sat.* Admission free.

& Partial access

⊖ Elephant & Castle

## Erith Museum

Erith Library, Walnut Tree Road, Erith, Kent. (0322) 336582.
Along with the Bexley Museum above, covers the London
borough of Bexley. Focuses on the Thames, Thames barges,
shipbuilding and other local river industries. Shop, full visitor
services and educational facilities. *Open 14.15-17.15 Mon &
Wed, 14.15-17.00 Sat.* Admission free.

& No access

⇌ Erith

## Forty Hall Museum

Forty Hill, Enfield, Middlesex. 081-363 8196. Three-storey mansion built about 1630 for City alderman and haberdasher Sir Nicholas Rainton (1569-1646). Covers the London borough of Enfield. Special collections include late 19thC and 20thC packaging and advertising material, and the designs, tools and furniture of Aesthetic Movement furniture-maker Ada Jacquin. Café, shop, limited visitor services and educational facilities. *Open 10.00-17.00 Tue-Sun.* Admission free.

⑤ Partial access – ground floor only.

⇒ Enfield Town (then bus 191, 231)

## Grange Museum of Community History

Neasden Roundabout, Neasden Lane, Willesden NW10. 081-908 7432. Cosy 18thC house, formerly a stableblock. Covers the London borough of Brent. Three period interiors including an Edwardian draper's shop rescued from a local street. Shop, full visitor services and educational facilities. *Open 12.00-17.00 Tue-Thur, 10.00-12.00 & 13.00-17.00 Sat.* Admission free.

⑤ Partial access – ground floor only.

⊖ Neasden

## Greenwich Borough Museum

Plumstead Library, 232 Plumstead High Street, Woolwich SE18. 081-855 3240. Covers the London borough of Greenwich. Shop, visitor services and limited educational facilities. *Open 14.00-19.00 Mon, 10.00-13.00 & 14.00-17.00 Tue & Thur-Sat.* Admission free.

⑤ Partial access – steps at entrance.

⇒ Plumstead

## Gunnersbury Park Museum

Gunnersbury Park, Acton W3. 081-992 1612. Former Rothschild country home, built in 1800 and set in large park. Covers the London boroughs of Hounslow and Ealing. Expect to see the hand printing press used by Chiswick Press; 17thC swords from the Hounslow sword factory; 19thC Rothschild family carriages; Victorian kitchens; large costume collection. See also Small Mansion Art Gallery (see page 168). Restaurant open weekends, shop, full visitor services and educational facilities. *Open Mar-Sep 13.00-17.00 Mon-Fri, 13.00-18.00 Sat, Sun*

*& Bank Hols; Oct-Feb 13.00-16.00 Mon-Sun.* Admission free.
🚾 Full access. Toilet.
⊖ Acton Town

**Hackney Museum**
Central Hall, Mare Street, Hackney E8. 081-986 6914. Museum of the London borough of Hackney, with its culturally diverse population reflected in many displays. Also contains a rare Anglo-Saxon logboat. Shop, full visitor services and educational facilities. *Open 10.00-12.30 & 13.30-17.00 Tue-Fri, 13.30-17.00 Sat.* Admission free.
🚾 Full access. Toilet.
⇞ Hackney Central

**Hampstead Museum**
Burgh House, New End Square, Hampstead NW3. 071-431 0144. Queen Anne house in the heart of old Hampstead. Café, shop, limited visitor services. *Open 12.00-17.00 Wed-Sun, 14.00-17.00 Bank Hols.* Admission free.
🚾 No access
⊖ Hampstead

*Hampstead Museum*

## Harrow Museum and Heritage Centre

Headstone Manor, Pinner View, Harrow, Middlesex. 081-861 2626. Medieval moated manor house with adjoining 16thC barn. Covers the London borough of Harrow. Café, shop, limited visitor services, full educational facilities. *Open 12.30-17.00 Wed-Fri, 10.30-17.00 Sat, Sun & Bank Hols. (Oct-Apr closes at dusk if earlier than 17.00)*. Admission free.
&#x267F; Full access. Toilet.
&#x2296; Harrow-on-the-Hill

## Hayes and Harlington Local History Collection

Hayes Library, Golden Crescent, Hayes, Middlesex. 081-473 2855. Three showcases of exhibits, one covering the Fairey Aviation Company. *Open 09.30-20.00 Mon, Tue & Thur, 09.30-17.30 Fri, 10.00-16.00 Sat*. Admission free.
&#x267F; Full access
&#x2748; Hayes & Harlington

## Hillingdon Borough Museum

Uxbridge Library, High Street, Uxbridge, Middlesex. (0895) 250600 (library), (0895) 250711 (borough museums officer). Changing exhibitions covering the London borough of Hillingdon. *Open 09.30-20.00 Mon-Thur, 09.30-17.30 Fri, 09.30-16.00 Sat*. Admission free.
&#x267F; Full access. Toilet.
&#x2296; Uxbridge

## Island History Trust

Island House, Roserton Street, Poplar E14. 071-987 6041. A collection of 4000 old photos depicting life on the Isle of Dogs. Limited visitor services, limited educational facilities. *Open 13.30-16.30 Tue, Wed & Fri*. Admission free.
&#x267F; No access
&#x2296; Mile End (then bus D7), Crossharbour DLR

## Kingston Museum and Heritage Centre

Wheatfield Way, Kingston-upon-Thames, Surrey. 081-546 5386. Covers the London borough of Kingston. Special feature on local photographer Eadweard Muybridge (1830-1904), the pioneer of movement photography. Also an art pottery collection especially strong in Martinware. Shop, limited visitor services. *Open 10.00-17.00 Mon-Sat*. Admission free.
&#x267F; Partial access – ground floor only.
&#x2748; Kingston

## Museum of Richmond

Old Town Hall, Whittaker Avenue, Richmond, Surrey. 081-
332 1141. Covers the Surrey bank of the Thames in
Richmond and Twickenham. Detailed models of Richmond
Palace and Shene Charterhouse. Shop, limited visitor services,
full educational facilities. *Open 11.30-17.00 Tue, 11.30-18.00
Wed-Fri, 10.00-17.00 Sat; also 13.30-16.00 Sun (May-Oct).*
Admission charge.
🚾 Full access. Toilet.
⊖ Richmond

## Museum of Soho

55 Dean Street W1. 071-439 4303.                              4 E2
Covers the central London district of Soho, home to London's
film and music industries and famous for its cosmopolitan
population and its numerous clubs and restaurants. Shop,
limited visitor services. *Phone for opening times.* Admission
charge.
🚾 Full access. Toilet.
⊖ Leicester Square

## Passmore Edwards Museum

Romford Road, Stratford E15. 081-519 4296. Covers the
London borough of Newham. Large collection of 18thC Bow
porcelain. Shop, limited visitor services, full educational
facilities. *Open 11.00-17.00 Wed-Fri, 13.00-17.00 Sat, 14.00-
17.00 Sun & Bank Hols.* Admission free.
🚾 Full access. Toilet.
⊖ Stratford

## Ragged School Museum

46-50 Copperfield Road, Bow E3. 081-980 6405. Housed in
three canalside warehouses, recording the history of the
ragged schools which provided free education for poor
children in the 19thC. Includes a reconstructed Victorian
classroom in which local children can often be seen having
lessons. Café, shop, full visitor services, full educational
facilities. *Open 10.00-17.00 Wed & Thur, 14.00-17.00 first
Sun of month.* Admission free.
🚾 No access
⊖ Mile End

## Redbridge Central Library Local History Room

Central Library, Clements Road, Ilford, Essex. 081-478 7145.
Covers the London borough of Redbridge. An exhibition in

words and pictures only – no objects. *Open 09.30-20.00 Tue-Fri, 09.30-16.00 Sat*. Admission free.
&#x267F; Full access. Toilet.
&#x21C8; Ilford

### Sutton Heritage Centre
Honeywood, Carshalton, Surrey. 081-773 4555. Along with Whitehall below, covers the London borough of Sutton. Café, shop, full visitor services and educational facilities. *Open 10.00-17.30 Tue-Sun & Bank Hols*. Admission charge.
&#x267F; Partial access – ground floor only.
&#x21C8; Carshalton

### Upminster Tithe Barn Agricultural and Folk Museum
Hall Lane, Upminster, Essex. (04024) 47535. Medieval thatched barn housing the Hornchurch and District Historical Society's collections, including old farm implements and tools. Limited visitor services. *Open Apr-Oct 14.00-18.00 first Sat & Sun in each month*. Admission free.
&#x267F; Partial access
&#x2296; Upminster

### Upminster Windmill
St Mary's Lane, Upminster, Essex. (0708) 44297. A well-preserved smock mill of 1803 with all its original machinery intact. Refreshments. *Open for guided tours Apr-Oct 14.00-18.00 third Sat & Sun in each month*. Admission free.
&#x267F; No access
&#x2296; Upminster

### Valence House Museum
Becontree Avenue, Dagenham, Essex. 081-592 4500. Early 17thC timber-framed manor house, partly moated. Covers the London borough of Barking and Dagenham. Fanshawe family portraits by Lely, Kneller and other 17thC and 18thC artists. Interior from local Edwardian chemist's shop. Shop, full visitor services and educational facilities. *Open 09.30-13.00 & 14.00-16.30 Mon-Fri*. Admission free.
&#x267F; Partial access – ground floor only. Toilet.
&#x21C8; Chadwell Heath

### Vestry House Museum
Vestry Road, Walthamstow E17. 081-509 1917. Covers the London borough of Waltham Forest. Unique Bremer car, built locally between 1892 and 1894, and reputedly the first British-made four-wheeled petrol-driven vehicle. Shop, limit-

*Vestry House Museum*

ed visitor services and educational facilities. *Open 10.00-13.00 & 14.00-17.30 Mon-Fri, to 17.00 Sat*. Admission free.
&#9635; Partial access – ground floor only.
&#9672; Walthamstow Central

**Wandsworth Museum**
Putney Library, Disraeli Road, Putney SW15. 081-871 7074. Covers the London borough of Wandsworth. Shop, limited visitor services. *Open 13.00-17.00 Mon-Wed, Fri & Sat*. Admission free.
&#9635; Partial access – ground floor only.
&#9672; East Putney

**Whitehall, Cheam**
1 Malden Road, Cheam, Sutton, Surrey. 081-643 1236. Weather-boarded house dating from 16thC. Along with Sutton Heritage Centre above, covers the London borough of Sutton. Displays on Henry VIII's Nonsuch Palace (demolished in the 17thC), Cheam School, Cheam pottery, and the 18thC artist and writer William Gilpin, the original Dr Syntax. Café, shop, limited visitor services and educational facilities. *Open Apr-Sep 14.00-17.30 Tue-Fri, Sun & Bank Hols, 10.00-17.30 Sat; Oct-Mar 14.00-17.30 Wed, Thur & Sun, 10.00-17.30 Sat*. Admission charge.
&#9635; Partial access – ground floor only.
&#9992; Cheam

**Wimbledon Society Museum**
Ridgway, Wimbledon SW19. No telephone. Shop. Limited visitor services, *Open 14.30-17.00 Sat*. Admission free.
&#9635; No access
&#9672; Wimbledon (then bus 93)

# Index to Local History Museums

**Barking**: Vestry House Museum 177

**Barnet**: Barnet Museum 171

**Bexley**: Bexley Museum 171, Erith Museum 172

**Bow**: Ragged School Museum 176

**Brent**: Grange Museum of Community History 173

**Bromley**: Bromley Museum 171

**Dagenham**: Vestry House Museum 177

**Ealing**: Gunnersbury Park Museum 173

**Enfield**: Forty Hall Museum 173

**Erith**: Erith Museum 172

**Greenwich**: Greenwich Borough Museum 173

**Hackney**: Hackney Museum 174

**Hampstead**: Hampstead Museum 175

**Haringey**: Bruce Castle Museum 172

**Harlington**: Hayes and Harlington Local History Collection 175

**Harrow**: Harrow Museum and Heritage Centre 175

**Hayes**: Hayes and Harlington Local History Collection 175

**Hillingdon**: Hillingdon Borough Museum,

Hayes/Harlington Local History Collection 175

**Hornchurch**: Upminster Tithe Barn Agricultural and Folk Museum 177, Upminster Windmill 177

**Hounslow**: Gunnersbury Park Museum 173

**Kingston-on-Thames**: Kingston Museum and Heritage Centre 175

**Newham**: Passmore Edwards Museum 176

**Redbridge**: Redbridge Central Library Local History Room 176

**Richmond**: Richmond Museum 176, Orleans House Gallery 166

**Soho**: Museum of Soho 176

**Southwark**: Cuming Museum 172, South London Art Gallery 169, Normanby College Library 68

**Sutton**: Sutton Heritage Centre 177, Whitehall (Cheam) 178

**Tower Hamlets**: Island History Trust 175

**Wandsworth**: Wandsworth Museum 178

**Wimbledon**: Wimbledon Society Museum 178, Wimbeldon Windmill Museum 106

# Index of Artists and Craftsmen

**Adam**, Robert, architect (*1728-92*) 123, 123, 129, 134, 135

**Aitchison**, George, architect (*1825-1910*) 125

**Alma-Tadema**, Sir Lawrence, painter (*1836-1912*) 126

**Altdorfer**, Albrecht, painter (*c1480-1538*) 147

**Antonello da Messina**, painter (*c1430-1479*) 147

**Auerbach**, Frank Helmuth, painter and draughtsman (*b.1931*) 154, 161

**Bacon**, John, painter (*1868-1914*) 154

**Baker**, Sir Herbert, architect (*1862-1946*) 9

**Banbury**, Henry William, painter (*1750-1811*) 90

**Barnsley**, William Edward, furniture maker (*b.1900*) 139

**Bassano**, Jacopo, painter (*c1517-1592*) 121

**Beechey**, Sir William, painter (*1753-1839*) 123, 141

**Bellini**, Giovanni, painter (*c1430-1516*) 147

**Blake**, William, painter (*1757-1827*) 154

**Boehm**, Joseph Edgar, painter (*1834-90*) 125

**Bol**, Ferdinand, painter (*1616-80*) 123

**Bomberg**, David, painter (*1890-1957*) 161

**Bonington**, Richard Parkes, painter (*1801-28*) 158

**Botticelli**, Sandro, painter (*1447-1510*) 145, 147

**Boucher**, Francois, painter (*1703-70*) 124, 157

**Boulle**, André-Charles, cabinet maker (*1642-1732*) 157

**Boyle**, Richard (Earl of Burlington), architect (*1694-1763*) 109

**Brangwyn**, Sir Frank, painter, (*1867-1956*) 139

**Braque**, Georges, painter (*1881-1963*) 155

**Bronzino**, Agnolo, painter (*1503-72*) 147

**Brown**, Lancelot Capability, landscape gardener (*1716-83*) 134

**Bruegel**, Pieter (The Elder), painter (*c1520-69*) 147

**Brueghel**, Jan (The First), painter (*1568-1625*) 136

**Brunel**, Marc Isambard, engineer (*1769-1849*) 19

**Brunel**, Isambard Kingdom, engineer (*1806-59*) 19

**Burne-Jones**, Sir Edward Coley, painter (*1833-98*) 126, 153, 155

**Caldecott**, Randolph, painter (*1846-86*) 125

**Campbell**, Colen, architect (*1676-1729*) 121, 127

**Campin**, Robert, painter (*1378-1444*) 147

**Canaletto**, Giovanni Antonio, painter (*1697-1768*) 132, 142, 151, 157, 158

**Canova**, Antonio, sculptor (*1757-1822*) 135

**Caravaggio**, Michelangelo Merisi da, painter (*1569-1610*) 141, 145, 147

**Cézanne**, Paul, painter (*1839-1906*) 141, 147, 155

**Chambers**, Sir William, architect (*1723-96*) 129

**Claude**, Gellée (Le Lorrain), painter (*1600-82*) 142, 145, 147, 157

**Clérisseau**, Charles Louis, painter (*1722-1820*) 132

**Clough**, Prunella, painter (*b.1919*) 141

**Constable**, John, painter (*1776-1837*) 103, 144, 145, 147, 152, 154

**Copley**, John, painter (*1737-1818*) 156

**Correggio**, Antonio Allegri da, painter (*1494-1534*) 118, 136

**Cortona**, Pietro da, painter and architect (*1596-1669*) 141

**Cotman**, John Sell, painter (*1782-1842*) 32

**Cranach**, the Elder (Lucas), painter (*1472-1553*) 118, 147

**Crane**, Walter, painter and illustrator (*1845-1915*) 126

**Crivelli**, Carlo, painter (*active 1457-93*) 147

**Cruikshank**, George, painter (*1792-1878*) 90

**Cruikshank**, Issac Robert, painter (*1789-1856*) 90

**Cuyp**, Aelbert, painter (*1620-91*) 124

**Dadd**, Richard, painter (*1819-87*) 140

**Dahl**, Michael, painter (*1656-1743*) 121

**Degas**, Edgar, painter (*1834-1917*) 141

**Delacroix**, Eugene, painter (*1798-1863*) 158

**Delaroche**, Hippolyte-Paul, painter (*1797-1856*) 147, 158

**Dickinson**, Frank, artist and designer (*1874-1961*) 127

**Dobson**, Frank, painter (*1888-1963*) 141

**Dolmetsch**, Arnold, musical instrument maker (*1858-1940*) 130, 131

**Domenichino**, Domenico Zampieri, painter (*1581-1641*) 147

**Dosso**, Dossi, painter (*1479/90-1542*) 147

**Dou**, Gerrit, painter (*1613-75*) 142, 147

**van Dyck**, Sir Anthony, painter (*1599-1641*) 121, 122, 123, 134, 136, 141, 142, 145, 147, 151, 157

**Elsheimer**, Adam, painter (*1578-1610*) 136

**Epstein**, Sir Jacob, painter (*1880-1959*) 161

**van Eyck**, Jan, painter (*before 1395-1441*) 145, 147

**Fetti**, Domenico, painter (*1589-1623*) 141
**Flaxman**, John, sculptor (*1755-1826*) 98
**Foster**, Norman, architect (*b.1935*) 143, 152
**Fragonard**, Jean-Honoré, painter (*1732-1806*) 157
**Freud**, Lucien, painter (*b.1922*) 154

**Gabo**, Naum, painter (*1890-1977*) 155
**Gainsborough**, Thomas, painter (*1727-88*) 57, 123, 125, 133, 141, 142, 144, 147, 151, 152, 154, 156, 157
**Gauguin**, Paul, painter (*1848-1903*) 141, 155
**Giacometti**, Alberto, sculptor (*1901-66*) 155
**Gibbons**, Grinling, carver (*1648-1721*) 118, 121
**Gibbs**, James, architect (*1682-1754*) 166
**Gillray**, James, painter (*1757-1815*) 90
**Gilpin**, William, artist and writer (*1724-1804*) 178
**Gimson**, Ernest, furniture maker (*1864-1919*) 139
**Giordano**, Luca, painter (*1634-1705*) 147
**Giotto**, (di Bondone), painter (*1266-1337*) 147
**Gossaert**, Jan de, ("Mabuse"), painter (*1478-1533*) 147

**Goya y Lucientes**, Francisco José de, painter (*1746-1828*) 136
**Graham**, George, clock- and watch-maker (*1673-1751*) 23
**Grant**, Duncan, painter (*1885-1978*) 141
**El Greco**, Domenikos, painter (*1541-1614*) 147
**Guardi**, Francesco, painter (*1712-93*) 157, 158
**Guercino**, Giovanni Francesco Barbieri, painter (*1591-1666*) 136

**Hals**, Frans, painter (*1581-1666*) 147, 157
**Harrison**, John, clock- and timepiece-maker (*1693-1776*) 24, 69
**Hayman**, Francis, painter (*1708-76*) 128
**Hayter**, Sir George, painter (*1792-1871*) 121
**Herman**, Josef, painter (*.b1911*) 161
**Highmore**, Joseph, painter (*1692-1780*) 156
**Hilliard**, Nicholas, painter (*1547-1619*) 155
**Hogarth**, William, painter (*1697-1764*) 119, 128, 132, 144, 147, 155, 156
**Holbein**, Hans (the Younger), painter (*1498-1543*) 147, 151
**Hooch**, Pieter de, painter (*1629-after 1684*) 147
**Hoogstraten**, Samuel van, painter (*1627-78*) 147
**Hudson**, Thomas, painter (*1701-79*) 156

**Johnson**, Cornelius, painter
(*1593-1661*) 130

**Jones**, Inigo, architect
(*1573-1652*) 10, 61

**Jordaens**, Jacques, painter
(*1593-1678*) 147

**Kent**, William, painter
(*1684-1748*) 110, 118,
121, 122

**Kneller**, Sir Godfrey,
painter (*1646-1723*) 57,
79, 107, 118, 121, 128,
154, 177

**Larkin**, William, painter
(*d.1619*) 130

**Lawrence**, Sir Thomas,
painter (*1769-1830*) 57,
132, 152, 154

**Leighton**, Frederic (Lord),
painter (*1830-96*) 125

**Lely**, Sir Peter, painter
(*1618-80*) 117, 121, 130,
134, 154, 177

**Leonardo da Vinci**, painter
(*1452-1519*) 145, 147,
152

**Liebermann**, Max, painter
(*1847-1935*) 161

**Linley Sambourne**,
Edward, caricaturist and
illustrator (*1844-1910*)
126

**Lotto**, Don Lorenzo, painter
(*c1480-1556*) 141

**Louthenbourg**, Philippe-
Jacques de, painter
(*1740-1812*) 60

**Mackmurdo**, Arthur, craftsman (*1851-1942*) 139

**Maclise**, Daniel, painter
(*1806-70*) 123

**Maes**, Nicolaes, painter
(*1634-93*) 147

**Manet**, Edouard, painter
(*1832-83*) 141

**Mantegna**, Andrea, painter
(*1431-1506*) 118, 147

**Martin brothers**, ceramists,
Guillaume (*d.1749*),
Julien (*d.1752*), Robert
(*d.1765*), Etienne-Simon
(*d.1770*) 46, 130

**Masaccio**, Tommaso di
Giovanni di Simone
Guidi, painter (*1401-28*)
147

**Matisse**, Henri, painter
(*1869-1954*) 155

**Michelangelo**, di Buonarotti
Lodovico Simoni,
painter (*1475-1564*) 103,
147, 152

**Mieris**, Willem van, painter
(*1662-1747*) 147

**Millais**, Sir John Everett,
painter (*1829-96*) 126,
169

**Modigliani**, Amedeo,
painter and sculptor
(*1884-1920*) 141

**Monet**, Claude, painter
(*1840-1926*) 141

**Moore**, Henry, sculptor
(*1898-1986*) 155

**Moretto**, da Brescia
(Alessandro Bonvicino),
painter (*c1498-1554*)
147

**Morgan**, William de
Frend de, painter and
novelist (*1839-1917*)
125, 128

**Morris**, William (junior),
designer (*1834-96*) 127,
138, 139

**Murillo**, Bartolomé Esteban, painter (*1617-82*) 142, 147, 157

**Muybridge**, Eadweard, photographer (*1830-1904*) 175

**Mytens**, Daniel, painter (*c1590-before 1648*) 130

**Nicholson**, Ben, painter (*1894-1982*) 141

**Nicholson**, Sir William, painter (*1872-1949*) 114

**North**, Marianne, painter (*1830-90*) 143

**Ostade**, Adriaen van, painter (*1610-85*) 124

**Palladio**, Andrea, architect (*1518-80*) 143

**Panini**, Giovanni Paolo, painter (*1691-1765*) 128

**Pater**, Jean-Baptiste-Joseph, painter (*1695-1736*) 124

**Paxton**, Sir Joseph, architect (*1801-65*) 25

**Perugino**, Pietro, painter (*c1450-1523*) 147

**Picasso**, Pablo, painter (*1881-1973*) 147, 155

**Piero della Francesca**, painter (*c1420-92*) 147

**Piero di Cosimo**, (Piero di Lorenzo), painter (*1462-1521*) 147

**Piombo**, Sebastiano del, painter (*c1485-1547*) 145, 147

**Piranesi**, Giovanni Battista, architect (*1720-28*) 132

**Pisanello**, (Antonio Pisano), painter (*1377-1455*) 147

**Pissarro**, Camille, painter (*1831-1903*) 141

**Pollaiuolo**, Antonio del, painter (*c1432-98*) 147

**Pollock**, Benjamin, toy theatre maker (*1856-1937*) 72

**Pontormo**, Jacopo da, painter (*1494-1557*) 147

**Poussin**, Nicolas, painter (*1594-1665*) 142, 147, 157

**Prinsep**, James, architect (*1799-1840*) 169

**Quare**, Daniel, clockmaker (*1648-1724*) 23

**Raeburn**, Sir Henry, painter (*1756-1823*) 141

**Ramsay**, Allan, painter (*1713-84*) 141, 156

**Raphael**, (Raffaello Sanzio), painter (*1483-1520*) 103, 145, 147, 156

**Rembrandt**, (Harmenszoon van Rijn), painter (*1606-69*) 123, 124, 142, 145, 147, 157

**Reni**, Guido, painter (*1575-1642*) 147

**Renoir**, Pierre-Auguste, painter (*1841-1919*) 141

**Reynolds**, Sir Joshua, painter (*1723-92*) 57, 103, 113, 123, 128, 132, 133, 142, 144, 147, 151, 152, 154, 155, 156, 157

**Romney**, George, painter (*1734-1802*) 123, 138, 141

**Rossetti**, Dante Gabriel, painter (*1828-82*) 155

**Rothko**, Mark, painter
  (*1903-70*) 155
**Roubiliac**, Louis François,
  painter (*1704-62*) 156
**Rowlandson**, Thomas,
  painter (*1756-1827*) 91
**Rubens**, Sir Peter Paul,
  painter (*1577-1640*) 122,
  136, 141, 142, 147, 157
**Ruskin**, John, painter (*1819-
  1900*) 127, 168
**Rysbrack**, John Michael,
  painter (*1693-1770*) 156

**Sargent**, John Singer,
  painter (*1856-1925*) 151,
  152, 155
**Sassetta**, (Stefano di
  Giovanni), painter
  (*1392-1450*) 147
**Seurat**, Georges de, painter
  (*1859-91*) 141, 147
**Sickert**, Walter, painter
  (*1860-1942*) 141
**Sisley**, Alfred, painter
  (*1839-99*) 141
**Smirke**, Robert, architect
  (*1781-1867*) 14
**Snyders**, Frans, painter
  (*1579-1657*) 122, 123
**Soane**, Sir John, architect
  (*1753-1837*) 9, 130, 132,
  142
**Spencer**, Sir Stanley, painter
  (*1891-1959*) 155, 168
**Steenwyck**, Henrick van,
  painter (*d.1649*) 118
**Stubbs**, George, painter
  (*1724-1806*) 144, 147
**Sutherland**, Graham,
  painter (*1903-80*) 169

**Teniers**, David, painter
  (*1610-90*) 121, 141, 147

**Thorneycroft**, Mary Alyce,
  sculptor (*1814-95*) 123
**Thornhill**, Sir James,
  painter (*1676-1734*) 80,
  118
**Tiepolo**, Gambattista,
  painter (*1696-1770*) 141,
  142
**Tijou**, Jean, ironworker
  (*active 1688-1712*) 118
**Tintoretto**, Jacopo Il,
  painter (*1578-94*) 147
**Titian**, (Tiziano Vecellio),
  painter (*1485-1576*) 118,
  145, 147, 157
**Tompian**, Thomas, clockmaker (*1639-1713*) 23
**Toulouse-Lautrec**, Henri
  de, painter (*1864-1901*)
  141
**Tura**, Cosimo, painter
  (*c1431-95*) 147
**Turner**, Joseph Mallord
  William, painter (*1775-
  1851*) 32, 60, 132, 144,
  145, 147, 152, 155

**Uccello**, Paulo, painter
  (*1397-1475*) 145, 147

**Vanbrugh**, Sir John,
  architect (*1664-1723*)
  118,
**Van de Veldes**, Esaias,
  painter (*1590-1630*) 61,
  124
**Van de Veldes**, Adraien,
  painter (*1636-72*) 61,
  124
**Van der Weyden**, Rogier,
  painter (*c1399-1464*)
  147
**Van Gogh**, Vincent, painter
  (*1853-90*) 141, 147, 155

**Velázquez**, Diego, painter (*1599-1660*) 136, 142, 145, 147, 157

**Venturi**, Robert, architect (*b.1925*) 144

**Vermeer**, Johannes, painter (*1632-75*) 123, 124, 147

**Veronese**, Paolo Caliari, painter (*1528-88*) 110, 147

**Verrio**, Antonio, interior designer, painter (*1639-1707*) 117, 118

**Voysey**, Charles Francis Annesley, furniture maker (*1857-1941*) 139

**Wain**, Ralph Louis, painter (*b.1911*) 140

**Warhol**, Andy, painter (*1930-87*) 154

**Waterhouse**, Alfred, architect (*1830-1905*) 63, 66

**Watteau**, Jean-Antoine, painter (*1684-1721*) 157

**Watts**, George Frederick, painter (*1817-1904*) 123, 126

**West**, Benjamin, painter (*1738-1820*) 125, 133, 156

**Whistler**, James Abbott McNeil, painter (*1834-1903*) 147

**Wilkins**, William, architect (*1773-1839*) 144

**Wilson**, Richard, painter (*1714-82*) 128, 147

**Wren**, Sir Christopher, architect (*1632-1723*) 69, 77, 80, 81, 118, 121, 128

**Wright of Derby**, Joseph, ceramist (*1734-97*) 109

**Zoffany**, Johann Joseph, painter (*1733-1810*) 125, 154

**Zurbáran**, Francisco, painter (*1598-1664*) 147

# Index

Accademia Italiana Delle Arti e
    Delle Arti Applicate  159
Alexander, Helene  28
Alexander of Tunis, Lord  31
Alexander, William  148
Alfred Dunhill Collection  7
All Hallows by the Tower
    Undercroft Museum  7
Amalgamated Engineering
    Union Collection  8
Angerstein, John Julius  170
Apsley, Lord  135
Architectural Association  159
Arkwright, Sir Richard  87
Artillery in the Rotunda,
    Museum of  47
Association of Illustrators  159

Baden-Powell House  8
Bank of England Museum  9
Bankside Gallery  160
Banqueting House  10
Barbican Art Gallery  160
Barnardo, Dr John  78
Barnet Museum  171
Barrie, James  71
Ben Uri Art Society  161
Bentham, Jeremy  97
Benton Fletcher, Major George
    114
Bethlem Royal Hospital
    Museum  140
Bethnal Green Museum of
    Childhood  11
Bexley Museum  171
Binning, Lady  114
Black Cultural Museum  12
Blake, William  53
Bligh, Admiral  49
Boleyn, Anne  39

Booth, General William  82
Boston Manor House  107
Bourgeois, Sir Francis  142
Boxing Museum  13
Bramah, Edward  90
Bramah Tea & Coffee Museum
    90
Brawne, Fanny  121
Bridgeman, Charles  127
British Dental Association
    Museum  13
British Museum  14
British Optical Association
    Foundation Collection  19
Bromley Museum  171
Bruce Castle Museum  172
Brunel's Engine House  19
Buchanan, Ken  13
Building Centre Gallery  161
Bunyan, John  53
Burlington, Earl of  109
Byron, Lord (George Gordon)
    32, 151

Cabinet War Rooms  20
Café Gallery  161
Camden Arts Centre  162
Canada House Gallery  162
Carew Manor  107
Carleton, Edward  108
Carlyle, Thomas  108
Carlyle's House  108
Carshalton House  108
Cavell, Edith  78
Charles I  10
Charles II  69, 77, 105
Charles Darwin Museum  108
Chartered Insurance Institute
    Museum  21
Chelsea Physic Garden  22

Chesterfield, Earl of 130
Chichester, Sir Francis 26
Child, Francis 129
Child, Robert 129
Chisendale Gallery 162
Chiswick House 109
Church Farm House Museum 110
Churchill, Sir Winston 20
Clink Prison 22
Clive, Robert 96
Clockmakers' Company Collection 23
Coleridge-Taylor, Samuel 13
Commonwealth Institute 24
Conan-Doyle, Sir Arthur 131
Conran, Sir Terence 27
Contemporary Applied Arts 162
Cook, Captain 52, 59, 60
Cooper, Henry 13
Coram, Captain Thomas 156
Courtauld Institute Galleries 140
Courtauld, Samuel 140
Craft Shop and Gallery 162
Crafts Council 163
Croydon Palace 112
Crystal Palace Museum 25
Cuming, Henry 172
Cuming Museum 172
Cuming, Richard 172
*Cutty Sark* 25

Darwin, Charles 67, 109
Darwin, Erasmus 109
David, Sir Percival 70
Design Centre 26
Design Museum 27
Dickens, Charles 71, 112, 156
Dickens House Museum 112
Dr Johnson's House 113
Dulwich Picture Gallery 142
Dunhill, Alfred 7

Edward III 105
Edward VIII 62

Elgar, Sir Edward 77
Embroiderer's Guild 118
Erith Museum 172

Fan Museum 28
Faraday, Michael 47
Fenton House 114
Fenton, James 114
Fenton, Philip 114
Flamsteed, Revered John 69
Flaxman Gallery 98
Flinders Petrie, W.M. 98
Florence Nightingale Museum 28
Forty Hall Museum 173
Franklin, Benjamin 81
Freud, Anna 115
Freud, Ernst 115
Freud Museum 115
Freud, Sigmund 115
Fulham Palace 116
Gabor, Dennis 88
Galerie Matisse 163
Garden History, Museum of 48
Gardner Wilkinson, Sir John 32
Garrick, David 91
Geffrye Museum 29
Geffrye, Sir Robert 29
George I 121
George II 127
George III 124, 125
Gielgud, Sir John 91
*Gipsy Moth IV* 25
Goethe-Institut 163
Goldsmiths' Hall 163
Grace, W.G. 47
Grange Museum of Community History 173
Grant, Robert 98
Greenwich Borough Museum 173
Gresham, Sir Thomas 129
Guards' Museum 30
Gunnersbury Park Museum 173

Hackney Museum 174

Hahnemann, Dr Samuel 31
Hahnemann Relics 31
Ham House 116
Hampstead Museum 174
Hampton Court Palace 117
Handel, George Frederic 77, 156
Harmsworth, Lord 113
Harrow Museum and Heritage Centre 175
Harrow School Old Speech Room Gallery 31
Haydn, Franz Joseph 77
Hayes and Harlington Local History Collection 175
Hayward Gallery 164
Heinz Gallery 143
Heinz, Henry II 143
Henry III 105
Henry V 105
Henry VII 105
Henry VIII 96, 117
Hillingdon Borough Museum 175
HMS *Belfast* 33
Hobbes, Thomas 151
Hogarth's House 119
Holmes, Sherlock 131
Holst, Gustav 77
Honourable Artillery Company, Museum of the 49
Horniman, Frederick MP 33
Horniman Museum 33
Howard, Henrietta 127

The Ice House, Holland Park 165
Imperial War Museum 34
Institute of Contemporary Arts (ICA) 164
Island History Trust 175
Iveagh Bequest 123
Iveagh, Earl of 123

Jacquin, Ada 173
Jagger, Mick 91
Jewel Tower 36

Jewish Museum 36
Johnson, Dr Samuel 81, 113
Johnston, Brian 47
Jones, Sir Horace 93
Josephine, Empress 136

*Kathleen & May* 37
Keats House 120
Keats, John 120, 151
Kensington Palace 121
Kenwood House 123
Kew Bridge Steam Museum 37
Kew Gardens Gallery 164
Kew Palace 124
Killigrew, Thomas 91
Kingston Museum and Heritage Centre 175
Kinnock, Neil MP 8

Leighton House 125
Linley Sambourne House 126
Lister, Baron Joseph 88
Little Holland House 127
Livesey Museum 38
Locke, John 151
London, Museum of 49
London Dungeon 39
London Fire Brigade Museum 40
London Gas Museum 40
London Museum of Jewish Life 41
London Toy & Model Museum 41
London Transport Museum 43
Lord, Thomas 46
Lovett, Edward 172

Madame Tussaud's 44
Mall Galleries 165
Mankind, Museum of 51
Mansfield, Earl of 123
Mantel, Ken 144
Mantel, Tija 144
Marble Hill House 127
Marianne North Gallery 143
Marlborough, Duke of 57

Marlborough, Lord 31
Markfield Beam Engine and
   Museum 45
Martinware Pottery Collection
   46
Marx, Karl 15
Massey Shaw, Sir Eyre 40
MCC Museum 46
Merrick, Joseph 78
Methodism, Museum of 52
Michael Faraday Museum 47
Monck, General 105
Moving Image, Museum of the
   53
Muhammad Ali 13
Museum of Artillery in the
   Rotunda 47
Museum of Garden History 48
Museum of the Honourable
   Artillery Company 49
Museum of London 49
Museum of Mankind 51
Museum of Methodism 52
Museum of the Moving Image
   53
Museum of the Order of St
   John 54
Museum of Richmond 176
Museum of the Royal
   Pharmaceutical Society of
   Great Britain 55
Museum of Soho 176
Museum of the United Grand
   Lodge of England 55
Museum of Zoology and
   Comparative Anatomy 98
Musical Museum 56

Napoleon Bonaparte, Louis
   135
Narwhal Inuit Art Gallery 144
National Army Museum 57
National Gallery 144
National Hearing Aid Museum
   58
National Maritime Museum 58
National Portrait Gallery 148
National Postal Museum 62

Natural History Museum 63
Nelson, Admiral Lord 59, 60,
   81, 105, 156
Newton, Sir Isaac 151
Nightingale, Florence 28, 68
Normanby College Library 68
North Woolwich Old Station
   Museum 68

Old Battersea House 128
Old Royal Observatory 68
Old St Thomas's Hospital
   Operating Theatre and
   Herb Garret 70
The Orangery 165
Order of St John, Museum of
   the 54
Orleans House Gallery 166
Osterley Park House 129

Passmore Edwards Museum
   176
Pasteur, Louis 88
Penn, William 8
Pepys, Samuel 72
Percival David Foundation of
   Chinese Art 70
Peter Pan Gallery 71
Petrie Museum of Egyptian
   Archaeology 98
Phillips, Reginald 62
Photographers' Gallery 166
Pitshanger Manor Museum
   130
Polish Institute and Sikorski
   Museum 71
Pollock's Toy Museum 72
Pope, Alexander 127
Prince Albert 103, 123
Prince Henry's Room 72
Public Record Office Museum
   73

The Queen's Gallery 151
Queen's House 61
Queen Charlotte 124, 125
Queen Charlotte's Cottage 125
Queen Henrietta Maria 61

Queen Mary  80, 118, 121
Queen Victoria  79, 103, 123

Raffles, Sir Stamford  52
Ragged School Museum  176
Rainton, Sir Nicholas  173
Ralegh, Sir Walter  96
Ranger's House  130
Redbridge Central Library
    Local History Room  176
Richard the Lionheart  39
Richardson, Samuel  81
Richmond, Museum of  176
Riesco Collection of Chinese
    Ceramics  73
Riesco, Raymond  73
Riverside Studios Gallery  166
Rock Circus  73
Roosevelt, President  21
Rothschild, Lord  133, 173
Royal Academy of Arts  152
Royal Air Force Museum  74
Royal Artillery Regimental
    Museum  76
Royal College of Art
    Exhibition Galleries  167
Royal College of Music
    Department of Portraits
    153
Royal College of Music
    Museum of Instruments  77
Royal College of Physicians
    153
Royal Festival Hall  167
Royal Hospital, Chelsea  77
Royal Institute of British
    Architects  168
Royal London Hospital
    Archives Centre and
    Museum  78
Royal Mews  79
Royal Military School of
    Music  79
Royal Naval College  80
Royal Pharmaceutical Society
    of Great Britain, Museum
    of the  55
Rugby Football Museum  80

Saatchi, Charles  154
Saatchi Collection  154
Sahib, Tippoo  136
St Bride's Crypt Exhibition  81
St John Ambulance Brigade  54
St Paul's Cathedral Crypt and
    Treasury  81
Salting, George  114
Salvation Army International
    Heritage Centre  82
Science Museum  82
Serpentine Gallery  168
Shakespeare Globe Museum
    88
Shakespeare, William  89
Shelley, Percy Bysshe  151
Sherlock Holmes Museum  131
The Showroom  168
Siddons, Sarah  91
Sikorski, General  71
Silver Studio Collection  89
Sir John Soane's Museum  132
Sloane, Sir Hans  14
Small Mansion Art Gallery
    168
Soho, Museum of  176
Soseki Museum in London
    132
Soseki, Natsume  132
South London Art Gallery  169
Spencer, Earl  133
Spencer House  133
Stephenson, George  87
Story of Telecommunications
    90
Strang Print Room  97
Suzannet, Comte de  113
Sutton Heritage Centre  177
Syon House  134

Tate Gallery  155
Tate, Sir Henry  155
Tea and Coffee (Bramah)
    Museum  90
Theatre Museum  91
Thomas Coram Foundation for
    Children  156
Tower Bridge Museum  92

Tower Hill Pageant 94
Tower of London 95
Tradescant, John junior 48
Tradescant, John senior 48
Trenchard, Lord 75
Treves, Sir Frederick 78
Tsunematsu, Sammy 133
Tussaud, Marie 44
Twining, Thomas 97
Twinings in the Strand 97

United Grand Lodge of
England, Museum of the
55
University College London
97
Upminster Tithe Barn
Agricultural and Folk
Museum 177
Upminster Windmill 177

Valence House Museum 177
Vavasour, Sir Thomas 116
Vestry House Museum 177
Victoria and Albert Museum
99
Vintage Wireless Museum 104

Wallace Collection 157
Wallace, Sir Richard 157
Wandsworth Museum 178
Wellcome, Sir Henry 87
Wellesley, Arthur 135

Wellington, Duke of 77, 81,
135, 136
Wellington, Lord 31
Wellington Museum 135
Wells, Gerald 104
Wesley, Charles 52, 138
Wesley, John 52, 137
Wesley's House 137
West, Dr Charles 71
Westminster Abbey Museum
104
Westminster Gallery 169
Whitechapel Art Gallery 170
Whitehall, Cheam 178
Wilkes, John 81
William III 80, 118, 121
William Morris Gallery 138
William Morris Society 139
Wimbledon Lawn Tennis
Museum 105
Wimbledon Society Museum
178
Wimbledon Windmill Museum
106
Windsor, Duke of 7
Winsor, Frederick 40
Woodlands Art Gallery 170
Wolfe Barry, Sir John 93
Wolsey, Cardinal 117
de Worde, Wynkyn 81

Zoology and Comparative
Anatomy, Museum of 98

# NICHOLSON

# MAPS

**KEY TO MAP PAGES**

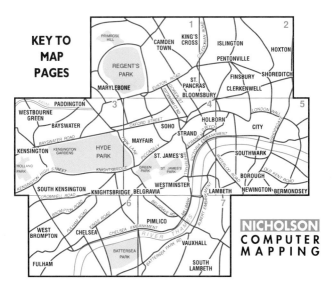

NICHOLSON
COMPUTER
MAPPING

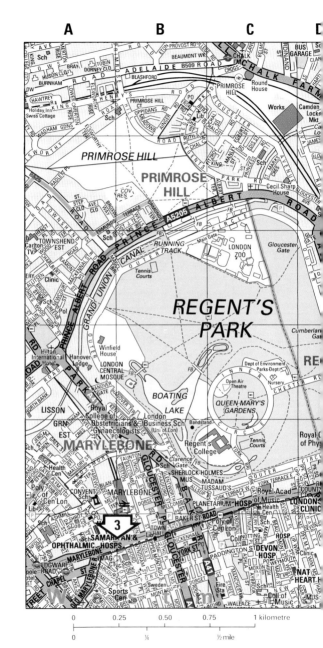

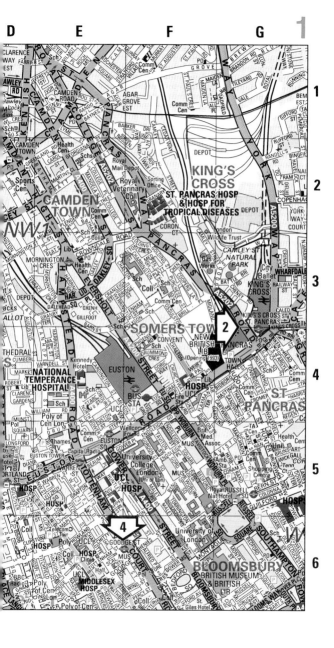

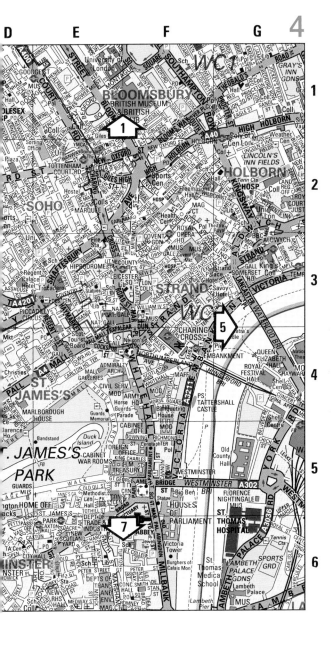

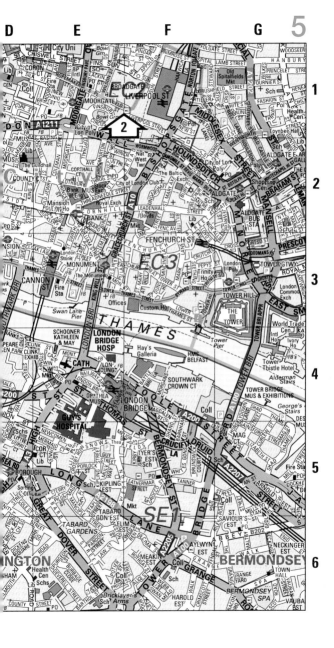

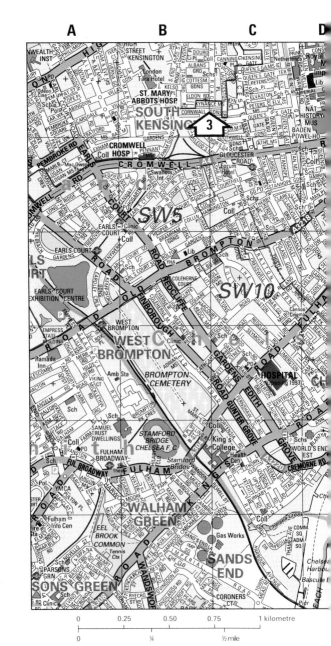

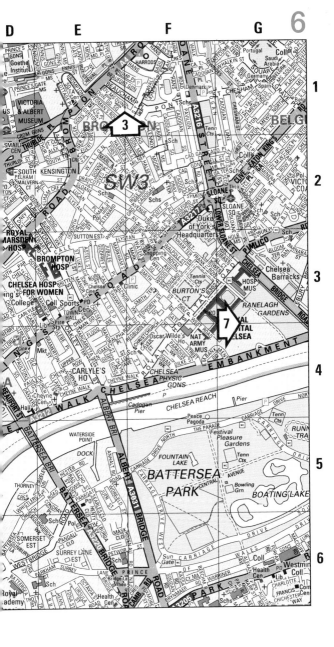

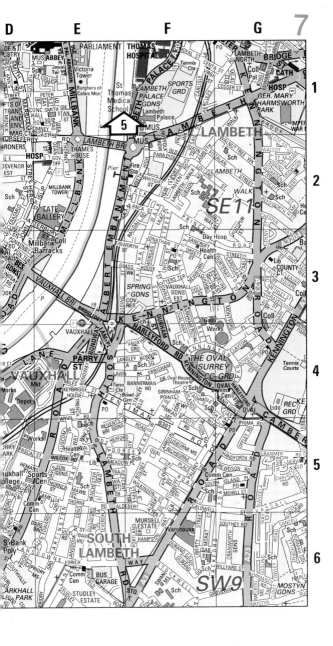

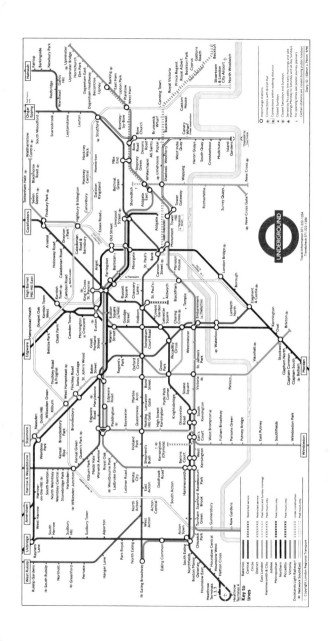